Kaplan Publishing are constantly fi[nding] **ways to make a difference to your studies and our exciting online resources really do offer something different to students looking for exam success.**

This book comes with free MyKaplan online resources so that you can study anytime, anywhere

Having purchased this book, you have access to the following online study materials:

CONTENT	ACCA (including FFA,FAB,FMA)		AAT		FIA (excluding FFA,FAB,FMA)	
	Text	Kit	Text	Kit	Text	Kit
iPaper version of the book	✓	✓	✓	✓	✓	✓
Interactive electronic version of the book	✓					
Progress tests with instant answers	✓		✓			
Mock assessments online			✓	✓		
Material updates	✓	✓	✓	✓	✓	✓
Latest official ACCA exam questions		✓				
Extra question assistance using the signpost icon*		✓				
Timed questions with an online tutor debrief using the clock icon*		✓				
Interim assessment including questions and answers	✓				✓	
Technical articles	✓	✓			✓	✓

* Excludes F1, F2, F3, FFA, FAB, FMA

How to access your online resources

Kaplan Financial students will already have a MyKaplan account and these extra resources will be available to you online. You do not need to register again, as this process was completed when you enrolled. If you are having problems accessing online materials, please ask your course administrator.

If you are already a registered MyKaplan user go to www.MyKaplan.co.uk and log in. Select the 'add a book' feature and enter the ISBN number of this book and the unique pass key at the bottom of this card. Then click 'finished' or 'add another book'. You may add as many books as you have purchased from this screen.

If you purchased through Kaplan Flexible Learning or via the Kaplan Publishing website you will automatically receive an e-mail invitation to MyKaplan. Please register your details using this email to gain access to your content. If you do not receive the e-mail or book content, please contact Kaplan Flexible Learning.

If you are a new MyKaplan user register at www.MyKaplan.co.uk and click on the link contained in the email we sent you to activate your account. Then select the 'add a book' feature, enter the ISBN number of this book and the unique pass key at the bottom of this card. Then click 'finished' or 'add another book'.

Your Code and Information

This code can only be used once for the registration of one book online. This registration and your online content will expire when the final sittings for the examinations covered by this book have taken place. Please allow one hour from the time you submit your book details for us to process your request.

Please scratch the film to access your MyKaplan code.

Please be aware that this code is case-sensitive and you will need to include the dashes within the passcode, but not when entering the ISBN. For further technical support, please visit www.MyKaplan.co.uk

AQ2013 Level 2

Basic Costing

REVISION KIT

KAPLAN

PUBLISHING

British Library Cataloguing-in-Publication Data

A catalogue record for this book is available from the British Library.

Published by:

Kaplan Publishing UK

Unit 2 The Business Centre

Molly Millar's Lane

Wokingham

Berkshire

RG41 2QZ

ISBN: 978-0-85732-891-5

© Kaplan Financial Limited, 2013

Printed and bound in Great Britain

CONTENTS

Features in this exam kit

In addition to providing a wide ranging bank of real exam style questions, we have also included in this kit:

- Paper specific information and advice on exam technique.

- Our recommended approach to make your revision for this particular subject as effective as possible.

You will find a wealth of other resources to help you with your studies on the AAT website:

www.aat.org.uk/

INDEX TO QUESTIONS AND ANSWERS

COST CLASSIFICATION

COST CODING

COST BEHAVIOUR

COSTING FOR INVENTORY AND WORK-IN-PROGRESS

COSTING FOR LABOUR

SPREADSHEETS AND VARIANCES

PAPER ENHANCEMENTS

We have added the following enhancements to the answers in this exam kit:

Key answer tips

Some answers include key answer tips to help your understanding of each question.

Tutorial note

Some answers include more tutorial notes to explain some of the technical points in more detail.

EXAM TECHNIQUE

- **Do not skip any of the material** in the syllabus.

- **Read each question** *very* carefully.

- **Double-check your answer** before committing yourself to it.

- Answer **every** question – if you do not know an answer to a multiple choice question or true/false question, you don't lose anything by guessing. Think carefully before you **guess**.

- If you are answering a multiple-choice question, **eliminate first those answers that you know are wrong**. Then choose the most appropriate answer from those that are left.

- **Don't panic** if you realise you've answered a question incorrectly. Getting one question wrong will not mean the difference between passing and failing

Computer-based exams – tips

- Do not attempt a CBA until you have **completed all study material** relating to it.

- On the AAT website there is a CBA demonstration. It is **ESSENTIAL** that you attempt this before your real CBA. You will become familiar with how to move around the CBA screens and the way that questions are formatted, increasing your confidence and speed in the actual exam.

- Be sure you understand how to use the **software** before you start the exam. If in doubt, ask the assessment centre staff to explain it to you.

- Questions are **displayed on the screen** and answers are entered using keyboard and mouse. At the end of the exam, you are given a certificate showing the result you have achieved.

- In addition to the traditional multiple-choice question type, CBAs will also contain **other types of questions**, such as number entry questions, drag and drop, true/false, pick lists or drop down menus or hybrids of these.

- In some CBAs you will have to type in complete computations or written answers.

- You need to be sure you **know how to answer questions** of this type before you sit the exam, through practice.

PAPER SPECIFIC INFORMATION

THE EXAM

FORMAT OF THE ASSESSMENT

Expect to see 17 tasks in the assessment, many of which will be split into more than one section and will cover all of the learning outcomes from the syllabus.

TIME ALLOWED

2 hours

PASS MARK

The pass mark for all AAT CBAs is 70%.

 Always keep your eye on the clock and make sure you attempt all questions!

DETAILED SYLLABUS

The detailed syllabus and study guide written by the AAT can be found at:

www.aat.org.uk/

KAPLAN'S RECOMMENDED REVISION APPROACH

QUESTION PRACTICE IS THE KEY TO SUCCESS

Success in professional examinations relies upon you acquiring a firm grasp of the required knowledge at the tuition phase. In order to be able to do the questions, knowledge is essential.

However, the difference between success and failure often hinges on your exam technique on the day and making the most of the revision phase of your studies.

The **Kaplan textbook** is the starting point, designed to provide the underpinning knowledge to tackle all questions. However, in the revision phase, poring over text books is not the answer.

The Kaplan workbook helps you consolidate your knowledge and understanding and is a useful tool to check whether you can remember key topic areas.

Kaplan pocket notes are designed to help you quickly revise a topic area, however you then need to practise questions. There is a need to progress to exam style questions as soon as possible, and to tie your exam technique and technical knowledge together.

The importance of question practice cannot be over-emphasised.

The recommended approach below is designed by expert tutors in the field, in conjunction with their knowledge of the examiner and the specimen assessment.

You need to practise as many questions as possible in the time you have left.

OUR AIM

Our aim is to get you to the stage where you can attempt exam questions confidently, to time, in a closed book environment, with no supplementary help (i.e. to simulate the real examination experience).

Practising your exam technique is also vitally important for you to assess your progress and identify areas of weakness that may need more attention in the final run up to the examination.

In order to achieve this we recognise that initially you may feel the need to practice some questions with open book help.

Good exam technique is vital.

THE KAPLAN BCST REVISION PLAN

Stage 1: Assess areas of strengths and weaknesses

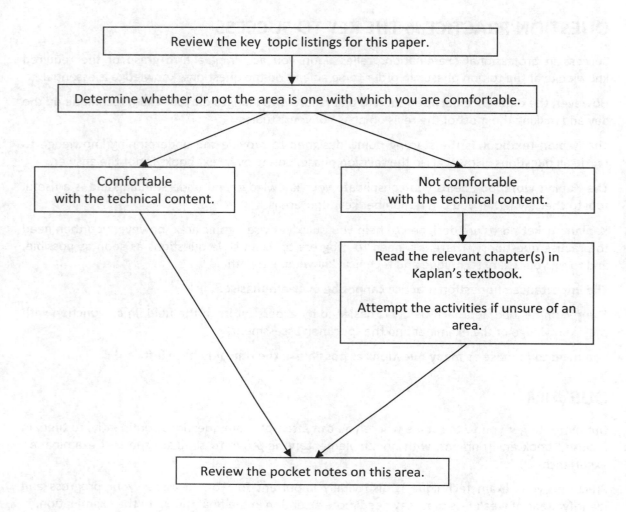

Stage 2: Practise questions

Follow the order of revision of topics as presented in this kit and attempt the questions in the order suggested.

Try to avoid referring to text books, notes and the model answer until you have completed your attempt.

Review your attempt with the model answer and assess how much of the answer you achieved.

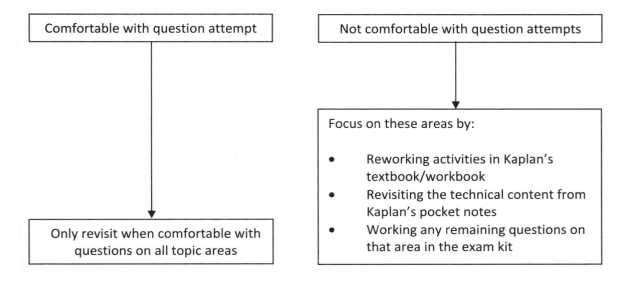

| Comfortable with question attempt | | Not comfortable with question attempts |

Focus on these areas by:

- Reworking activities in Kaplan's textbook/workbook
- Revisiting the technical content from Kaplan's pocket notes
- Working any remaining questions on that area in the exam kit

Only revisit when comfortable with questions on all topic areas

Stage 3: Final pre-exam revision

We recommend that you **attempt at least one two hour mock examination** containing a set of previously unseen exam standard questions.

Attempt the mock CBA online in timed, closed book conditions to simulate the real exam experience.

Section 1

PRACTICE QUESTIONS

COST CLASSIFICATION

FINANCIAL AND MANAGEMENT ACCOUNTING

1   FAMA

The table below lists some of the characteristics of financial accounting and management accounting systems.

Indicate two characteristics for each system by putting a tick in the relevant column of the table below.

Characteristic	Financial Accounting	Management Accounting
• Have to be produced annually		
• Analyses historic events to help produce forecasts		
• Is always produced using accounting standards		
• Is produced on an ad hoc basis when required		

2 FINANCIAL AND MANAGEMENT

The table below lists some of the characteristics of financial accounting and management accounting systems.

Indicate two characteristics for each system by putting a tick in the relevant column of the table below.

Characteristic	Financial Accounting	Management Accounting
• Must be presented as specified by the Companies Act and accounting standards		
• Helps managers run the business on a day-to-day basis		
• Used as the basis for the calculation of the organisation's tax charge		
• Can include anything that managers feel is useful for the business		

3 MAFA

The table below lists some of the characteristics of financial accounting and management accounting systems.

Indicate two characteristics for each system by putting a tick in the relevant column of the table below.

Characteristic	Management Accounting	Financial Accounting
• It is based on past events		
• Its purpose is to provide information for managers		
• It is based on future events		
• It complies with company law and accounting rules		

4   FEATURES

The table below lists some features typical of financial accounting and management accounting systems.

Indicate which feature applies to which system by putting a tick in the relevant column of the table below.

Feature	Financial Accounting	Management Accounting
• Analysis of profit by cost centre		
• Statement of profit or loss using format as dictated by accounting standards and company law		
• Cash flow forecasts		
• Cost per unit calculation		

COST AND PROFIT CENTRES

5   JEREMY

Jeremy operates a business that bakes bread. These are made in a small bakery and then sent to Jeremy's shop, where they are sold. Jeremy also has a small office where all of the administration is undertaken.

Identify whether the following departments are likely to be profit or cost centres by putting a tick in the relevant column of the table below.

Department	Cost centre	Profit centre
• Bakery		
• Shop		
• Office		

6   PRINT PLC

Print plc is a large company that prints and sells books. It is split into three divisions – binding, shops and marketing. The binding department prints the books. These are then either transferred to Print's chain of shops where they are sold to the public, or sold direct from the binding department to corporate clients. The marketing department produces all of Print's advertising.

Identify whether the following departments are likely to be profit or cost centres by putting a tick in the relevant column of the table below.

Department	Cost centre	Profit centre
• Binding		
• Shops		
• Marketing		

7   HOOCH PLC

Identify whether the following definitions are of be profit, cost, or investment centres by putting a tick in the relevant column of the table below.

Department	Cost centre	Profit centre	Investment centre
• Hooch's manager has no responsibility for income or asset purchases and disposals.			
• Hooch's manager is assessed on the profitability of their department, as well as how effectively they have controlled their assets.			
• Hooch's manager is responsible for income and expenditure of their department only.			

CLASSIFYING COSTS BY ELEMENT (MATERIALS, LABOUR OR OVERHEADS)

8   VVV LTD

VVV Ltd manufactures toy planes.

Classify the following costs by element (direct materials, direct labour or overheads) by putting a tick in the relevant column of the table below.

Cost	Direct Materials	Direct Labour	Overheads
• Paint used on the planes			
• Depreciation of the machines used in the factory			
• Oil used on the machines in the factory			
• Salary of worker assembling the planes			

9   TRIP LTD

Trip Ltd is a company that provides travel insurance.

Classify the following costs by element (materials, labour or other expenses) by putting a tick in the relevant column of the table below.

Cost	Materials	Labour	Overheads
• Wages of the insurance clerks dealing with claims			
• Rent of the office			
• Paper used to print off insurance policies			
• Salary of the office manager			

10   BMI LTD

BMI Ltd is a Gym.

Classify the following costs by element (materials, labour or overheads) by putting a tick in the relevant column of the table below.

Cost	Materials	Labour	Overheads
• Personal trainers wages			
• Electricity cost			
• Depreciation of gym equipment			
• Salary of the gym manager			

11   ACC LTD

ACC Ltd is a company that provides accountancy and audit services.

Classify the following costs by element (materials, labour or other expenses) by putting a tick in the relevant column of the table below.

Cost	Materials	Labour	Overheads
• Wages of the accountants			
• Office water rates			
• Depreciation of the computers used by the accountants			
• Paper used by the accountants in their audits			

CLASSIFYING COSTS BY NATURE (DIRECT OR INDIRECT)

12   LOVELOX LTD

Lovelox Ltd operates a chain of hairdressing salons.

Classify the following costs by nature (direct or indirect) by putting a tick in the relevant column of the table below.

Cost	Direct	Indirect
• Shampoo used on hair		
• Depreciation of salons		
• Wages of salon cleaner		
• Wages of hair stylists		

13 RUSSETT LTD

Russett Ltd is in business as a tablet computer manufacturer.

Classify the following costs by nature (direct or indirect) by putting a tick in the relevant column of the table below.

Cost	Direct	Indirect
• Glass used to make tablets		
• Insurance of factory		
• Wages of workers assembling tablets		
• Cost of entertaining corporate clients		

14 SCOTLAND LTD

Scotland Ltd makes sports clothing.

Classify the following costs by nature (direct or indirect) by putting a tick in the relevant column of the table below.

Cost	Direct	Indirect
• Cleaners' wages		
• Advertising expense		
• Material used in production		
• Production manager's wages		
• Machinist wages		

15 DIRECT OR INDIRECT

Classify the following costs by nature (direct or indirect) by putting a tick in the relevant column of the table below.

Cost	Direct	Indirect
• Chargeable hour for a lawyer		
• Machine hire for a building contractor in a long term contract		
• Electricity for a garden centre		
• Audit fee for a restaurant		

16 DIRECT COSTS ARE CONVENTIONALLY DEEMED TO:

A   be constant in total when activity levels alter

B   be constant per unit of activity

C   vary per unit of activity where activity levels alter

D   vary in total when activity levels remain constant

CLASSIFYING COSTS BY FUNCTION (PRODUCTION, ADMINISTRATION OR SELLING AND DISTRIBUTION)

17 NOOGLE LTD

Noogle Ltd produces microwaveable ready meals.

Classify the following costs by function (production, administration, or selling and distribution) by putting a tick in the relevant column of the table below.

Cost	Production	Administration	Selling and distribution
• Purchases of plastic for ready meal containers			
• Depreciation of sales department's delivery lorries			
• Insurance of office computers			
• Salaries of production workers			

18 HEAVING LTD

Heaving Ltd produces exercise equipment.

Classify the following costs by function (production, administration, or selling and distribution) by putting a tick in the relevant column of the table below.

Cost	Production	Administration	Selling and distribution
• Paper used to print off sales invoices			
• Metal used to make weights and bars			
• Depreciation of sales person's vehicle			
• Repairs to machine in factory			

19 KORMA PLC

Classify the following costs by function (production or non-production) by putting a tick in the relevant column of the table below.

Cost	Production	Administration	Selling and distribution	Finance
• Direct materials				
• Sales director salary				
• Head office printer ink				
• Direct labour				
• Bank charges				

20 GREOGRIAN LTD

Classify the following costs by function and nature by putting a tick in the relevant column of the table below.

Cost	Production – direct costs	Production – overheads	Selling overheads
• Direct labour			
• Power used in production machinery			
• Training costs for new employees in advertising			
• Insurance for sales team cars			
• Insurance for production machinery			

CLASSIFYING COSTS BY BEHAVIOUR (FIXED, VARIABLE OR SEMI-VARIABLE)

21 QUARK LTD

Quark Ltd runs a bar.

Classify the following costs by their behaviour (fixed, variable, or semi-variable) by putting a tick in the relevant column of the table below.

Cost	Fixed	Variable	Semi-variable
• Bar manager's salary			
• Alcohol used to make drinks			
• Rent of bar			
• Telephone costs, including standard line rental charge			

22   MORN LTD

Morn Ltd is a manufacturer of chairs and stools.

Classify the following costs by their behaviour (fixed, variable, or semi-variable) by putting a tick in the relevant column of the table below.

Cost	Fixed	Variable	Semi-variable
• Wood used in production			
• Advertising manager's salary			
• Electricity costs which include a standing charge			
• Labour costs paid on a piecework basis			

23   STEPPED FIXED COST

Which of the following would usually be classed as a stepped fixed cost?

A   Supervisor's wages

B   Raw materials

C   Rates

D   Telephone

24   BRAETAK LTD

Classify the following costs by their behaviour (fixed, variable, or semi-variable) by putting a tick in the relevant column of the table below.

Cost	Fixed	Variable	Semi-variable
• Rent			
• Wages of production workers paid on an hourly basis			
• Wages of production workers paid by a piece rate method			
• Sales staff paid a basic wage plus commission for each unit sold			

25 ODO LTD

Odo Ltd is a manufacturer of clothes.

Classify the following costs by their behaviour (fixed, variable, or semi-variable) by putting a tick in the relevant column of the table below.

Cost	Fixed	Variable	Semi-variable
• Material used in the production process			
• Safety review fee for the year			
• Electricity costs which include a standing charge			
• Labour costs paid on a per unit basis			

26 DEFINITIONS

Identify the following costs by their behaviour (fixed, variable, or semi-variable) by putting a tick in the relevant column of the table below.

Behaviour	Fixed	Variable	Semi-variable	Stepped cost
• This type of cost increases in direct proportion to the amount of units produced				
• This type of cost has a fixed and a variable element				
• This type of cost remains constant despite changes in output				
• This type of cost is fixed within a certain range of output				

27 COSTS

Match a graph to each of the following costs by labelling each graph with a letter (A-E):

(a) Variable cost per unit

(b) Total fixed cost

(c) Stepped fixed costs

(d) Total variable cost

(e) Semi-variable cost

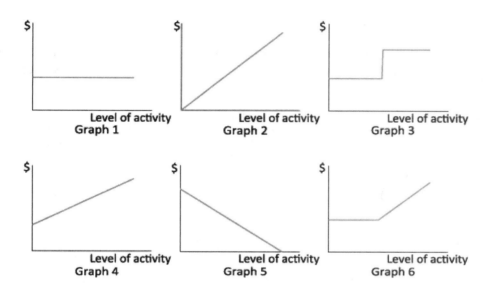

COST CODING

28 BYTES LTD

Sale Limited operates an IT consultancy business and uses a coding system for its elements of cost (materials, labour or overheads) and then further classifies each element by nature (direct or indirect cost) as below.

So, for example, the code for direct materials is A100.

Element of Cost	Code	Nature of Cost	Code
Materials	A	Direct	100
		Indirect	200
Labour	B	Direct	100
		Indirect	200
Overheads	C	Direct	100
		Indirect	200

Code the following costs, extracted from invoices and payroll, using the table below.

Cost	Code
• Salary of trainee IT consultant	
• Planning costs to renew lease of the office	
• Wages of the office manager	
• Cleaning materials used by cleaner	

29 SIMPLYFLY LTD

Simplyfly Ltd, a US manufacturer of aeroplanes, uses a numerical coding structure based on one profit centre and three cost centres as outlined below. Each code has a sub-code so each transaction will be coded as ***/***

Profit/Cost Centre	Code	Sub-classification	Sub-code
Sales	100	US Sales	100
		Overseas Sales	200
Production	200	Direct Cost	100
		Indirect Cost	200
Administration	300	Direct Cost	100
		Indirect Cost	200
Selling and marketing	400	Direct Cost	100
		Indirect Cost	200

Code the following revenue and expense transactions, which have been extracted from purchase invoices, sales invoices and payroll, using the table below.

Transaction	Code
• Office heating	
• Oil for the machines in production	
• Sale to New York (US)	
• Sale to Germany	
• Fabric for seat covers	
• Factory canteen wages	

30   BUNTON LTD

Bunton Ltd, a manufacturer of bottled water, uses a numerical coding structure based on one profit centre and three cost centres as outlined below. Each code has a sub-code so each transaction will be coded as ***/***

Profit/Cost Centre	Code	Sub-classification	Sub-code
Revenue	100	Direct Revenue	100
		Indirect Revenue	200
Production	200	Direct Cost	100
		Indirect Cost	200
Administration	300	Direct Cost	100
		Indirect Cost	200
Selling and Distribution	400	Direct Cost	100
		Indirect Cost	200

Code the following revenue and expense transactions, which have been extracted from purchase invoices, sales invoices and payroll, using the table below.

Transaction	Code
• Petrol for lorries	
• Warehouse rent	
• Sales of water	
• Rent received	
• Materials to make plastic bottles	

31   NAYULZ LTD

Nayulz Limited operates a nail salon and uses a coding system for its elements of cost (materials, labour or overheads) and then further classifies each element by nature (direct or indirect cost) as below. So, for example, the code for direct materials is A100.

Element of Cost	Code	Nature of Cost	Code
Materials	A	Direct	100
		Indirect	200
Labour	B	Direct	100
		Indirect	200
Overheads	C	Direct	100
		Indirect	200

Code the following costs, extracted from invoices and payroll, using the table below.

Cost	Code
• Salary of trainee nail technician	
• Legal costs against a customer who refused to pay	
• Wages of salon cleaner	
• Heat and light for salon	
• Nail polish used on customers	

32   INDIANA LTD

Indiana Ltd cleaning services provide contract cleaning to schools, hotels, hospitals and offices.

They have 3 profit centres.

The company analysis sales depending on the type of business they are cleaning.

Indiana Ltd uses a numerical coding structure based on profit centres and business type.

Profit centre	Code
Kiveton	100
Whitby	110
Birmingham	120

Business type	Code
School	200
Hotels	210
Hospitals	220
Offices	230

For example, expenses for the Whitby office would be coded 110/230.

Code the following revenue and expense transactions, which have been extracted from sales invoices and payroll, using the table below.

Location	Code
• Whitewell High School (Kiveton)	
• White Swan Hotel (Kiveton)	
• Worcester Royal Hospital (Birmingham)	
• Dudley Council Offices (Birmingham)	
• Browns Hotel (Birmingham)	
• Dunn and Musgrove Offices (Whitby)	

33 GREENFINGERS

Greenfingers Ltd runs a garden centre and uses a coding system for its elements of cost (materials, labour or overheads) and then further classifies each element by nature (direct or indirect cost) as below. So, for example, the code for direct materials is A100.

Element of Cost	Code	Nature of Cost	Code
Materials	A	Direct	100
		Indirect	200
Labour	B	Direct	100
		Indirect	200
Overheads	C	Direct	100
		Indirect	200

Code the following costs, extracted from invoices and payroll, using the table below.

Cost	Code
• Purchase of seeds used to grow plants for resale	
• Accountancy fees for preparation of year end accounts	
• Wages of gardeners who maintain the plants to be sold	
• Cleaning materials used by cleaner	
• Salary of office manager	

COST BEHAVIOUR

NARRATIVE STYLE QUESTIONS

34 BUNGLE LTD

Bungle Ltd usually produces 9,000 units but is planning to increase production to 14,000 units during the next period.

Identify the following statements as either true or false by putting a tick in the relevant column of the table below.

Statement	True	False
• Total variable costs will decrease		
• Total fixed costs will remain the same		
• The variable cost per unit will remain the same		
• The fixed cost per unit will increase		

35 TF

Identify the following statements as either true or false by putting a tick in the relevant column of the table below.

Statement	True	False
• Variable costs change directly with changes in activity		
• Fixed costs change directly with changes in activity		
• Stepped costs are fixed within a set range of output		

36 FIXED OR VARIABLE

Identify the following costs as either Fixed or variable by putting a tick in the relevant column of the table below.

Cost	Fixed	Variable
• Direct materials		
• Power used in production machinery		
• Training costs for new employees in production		
• Insurance for sales cars		
• Insurance for machinery		
• Sales commission		

CALCULATION QUESTIONS

37 MARIO PLC

Identify the type of cost behaviour (fixed, variable or semi-variable) described in each statement by putting a tick in the relevant column of the table below.

Statement	Fixed	Variable	Semi-variable
• Costs are £75,000, which is made up of a fixed charge of £45,000 and a further cost of £3 per unit at 7,000 units.			
• Costs are £75 per unit when 1,000 units are made and £15 per unit when 5,000 units are made.			
• Costs are £65 per unit regardless of the number of units made.			

38   TRIGEORGIS PLC

Identify the type of cost behaviour (fixed, variable or semi-variable) described in each statement by putting a tick in the relevant column of the table below.

Statement	Fixed	Variable	Semi-variable
• Costs are £50,000 in total regardless of the number of units made.			
• Costs are £50,000 in total when 2,500 units are made and £80,000 when 4,000 units are made.			
• Costs are £7 per unit when 1,000 units are made and £6 per unit when 2,000 units are made.			

39   JEEPERS LTD

Indicate whether the following costs are direct or not by putting a tick in the relevant column of the table below.

Cost	Yes	No
• Materials used in production		
• Piecework labour costs		
• Salary of chief executive		

Jeepers Ltd makes a single product. At a production level of 15,000 units, the company has the following costs:

Materials	37,500 kilos at £14.00 per kilo
Labour	7,500 hours at £16.00 per hour
Overheads	£570,000

Complete the table below to show the unit product cost at the production level of 15,000 units.

Element	Unit Product Cost
Materials	£
Labour	£
Direct cost	£
Overheads	£
Total	£

40 TWO-PART PLC

Complete the table below showing fixed costs, variable costs, total costs and unit cost at the different levels of production

Units	Fixed Costs	Variable Costs	Total Costs	Unit Cost
1500	£15,000	£6,000	£21,000	£14
2,000	£	£	£	£
2,500	£	£	£	£
3,000	£	£	£	£

Using your calculations above, identify the following statements as either true or false by putting a tick in the relevant column of the table below:

Statement	True	False
• The cost per unit increases as output increases due to the total variable costs increasing.		
• The cost per unit does not alter as output increases because the total cost increases.		
• The cost per unit decreases as output increases because the fixed costs are spread over more units.		

41 GLORIA LTD

Gloria Ltd is costing a single product which has the following cost details:

Variable Costs per unit

Materials	£2
Labour	£3
Royalties	£0.50

Total Fixed Costs

Production overhead	£80,000
Sales and distribution	£90,000

Complete the following total cost and unit cost table for a production level of 20,000 units.

Element	Unit cost	Total Cost for 20,000 units
Variable production costs	£	£
Fixed production costs	£	£
Total production cost	£	£

42 METRIC LTD

Metric Ltd makes a single product and for a production level of 24,000 units has the following cost details:

	Per unit	Cost
Materials	0.5kg	£10/kilo
Labour	1.5hrs	£8/hour
Overheads		£48,000

Complete the table below to show the unit cost at the production level of 24,000 units.

Element	Unit Cost	Total cost
Materials	£	£
Labour	£	£
Overheads	£	£
Total	£	£

43 VINNY LTD

Vinny Ltd is a commercial laundrette below are the costings for 15,000 units:

Variable Costs

Materials	£75,000
Labour	£120,000

Fixed Costs

Production overhead	£100,000

Complete the following total cost and unit cost table for a REVISED production level of 20,000 units.

Element	Unit cost	Total cost
Materials	£	£
Labour	£	£
Overheads	£	£
Total	£	£

44   GREEGY LTD

Greegy Ltd makes a single product and for a production level of 40,000 units has the following cost details:

Materials	20,000kg	at £10/kilo
Labour	10,000hrs	at £6/hour
Fixed Overheads		£60,000

Complete the table below to show the unit cost at a REVISED production level of 30,000 units.

Element	Unit cost	Total cost
Materials	£	£
Labour	£	£
Overheads	£	£
Total	£	£

45   SIMON LTD

Simon Ltd is costing a single product which has the following cost details

Variable costs	*Per unit*	*Cost*
Materials	20g	£0.10/g
Labour	0.5hrs	£6/hour
Patent		£2/unit

Total Fixed Costs	
Production overhead	£80,000
Administration overhead	£60,000
Sales and distribution	£50,000

Complete the following total cost and unit cost table for a production level of 20,000 units.

Element	Total Cost for 20,000 units	Unit Cost
Direct costs	£	£
Production overhead	£	£
Non production overhead	£	£
Total costs	£	£

46 OLSEN LTD

Olsen Ltd is costing a single product which has the following cost details:

Variable costs	Per unit
Materials	£12
Labour	£17
Total Fixed Costs	
Production overhead	£80,000
Administration overhead	£40,000

Complete the following total cost and unit cost table for a production level of 80,000 units.

Element	Total Cost	Unit cost
Materials	£	£
Labour	£	£
Production Overheads	£	£
Administration Overheads	£	£
Total	£	£

47 FLAKEWAY LTD

Flakeway Ltd makes a single product and for a production level of 24,000 units has the following cost details:

Materials	6,000kg	at £20/kilo
Labour	8,000hrs	at £12/hour
Fixed Overheads		£48,000

Complete the table below to show the unit cost at the production level of 24,000 units.

Element	Total Cost	Unit cost
Materials	£	£
Labour	£	£
Production Overheads	£	£
Administration Overheads	£	£
Total	£	£

48   CORONATION LTD

Coronation Ltd is costing a single product which has the following cost details

Variable costs	Per unit	Cost
Materials	50g	£10/kg
Labour	1hr	£6/hour

Total Fixed Costs

Production overhead	£40,000
Administration overhead	£20,000
Sales and distribution	£25,000

Complete the following total cost and unit cost table for a production level of 5,000 units.

Element	Total Cost for 5,000 units	Unit Cost
Direct costs	£	£
Production overhead	£	£
Non production overhead	£	£
Total costs	£	£

49   IRONSIDE LTD

Ironside Ltd makes a single product and for a production level of 40,000 units has the following cost details:

Materials	60,000kg	at £20/ kilo
Labour	40,000hrs	at £12/hour
Fixed Overheads		£117,000

Complete the table below to show the unit cost at the production level of 45,000 units.

Element	Unit Cost	Total cost
Materials	£	£
Labour	£	£
Overheads	£	£
Total	£	£

MANUFACTURING ACCOUNTS

50 MANU LTD

Reorder the following costs into a manufacturing account format on the right side of the table below for the year ended 31 December.

	£		£
Closing Inventory of Work in Progress	52,000		
Direct Labour	140,000		
Opening Inventory of Raw Materials	50,000		
Closing Inventory of Finished Goods	61,000		
Closing Inventory of Raw Materials	65,000		
Manufacturing Overheads	85,000		
COST OF GOODS SOLD	322,000		
MANUFACTURING COST	330,000		
Purchases of Raw Materials	120,000		
Opening Inventory of Work in Progress	48,000		
Opening Inventory of Finished Goods	57,000		
DIRECT COST	245,000		
DIRECT MATERIALS USED	105,000		
COST OF GOODS MANUFACTURED	326,000		

51   CHARTERIS LTD

Reorder the following costs into a manufacturing account format on the right side of the table below for the year ended 31 July.

	£		£
COST OF GOODS MANUFACTURED	188,000		
Opening Inventory of Work in Progress	12,000		
Opening Inventory of Raw Materials	10,000		
COST OF GOODS SOLD	186,000		
Closing Inventory of Finished Goods	20,000		
Closing Inventory of Raw Materials	12,000		
Manufacturing Overheads	45,000		
MANUFACTURING COST	191,000		
Purchases of Raw Materials	60,000		
Opening Inventory of Finished Goods	18,000		
DIRECT COST	146,000		
Direct Labour	88,000		
Closing Inventory of Work in Progress	15,000		
DIRECT MATERIALS USED	58,000		

52   KRATOS LTD

Reorder the following costs into a manufacturing account format on the right side of the table below for the year ended 31 May. Enter the correct figures for the costs in bold that are not provided.

	£		£
DIRECT COST			
Closing Inventory of Raw Materials	20,000		
Closing Inventory of Work in Progress	20,000		
Opening Inventory of Finished Goods	60,000		
Direct Labour	194,000		
Closing Inventory of Finished Goods	50,000		
Manufacturing Overheads	106,000		
Purchases of Raw Materials	100,000		
Opening Inventory of Work in Progress	16,000		
COST OF GOODS SOLD			
DIRECT MATERIALS USED			
Opening Inventory of Raw Materials	14,000		
MANUFACTURING COST			
COST OF GOODS MANUFACTURED			

53 SVEN LTD

Reorder the following costs into a manufacturing account format on the right side of the table below for the year ended 31 May. Enter the correct figures for the costs in bold that are not provided.

	£		£
Closing Inventory of Work in Progress	10,000		
Direct Labour	97,000		
Opening Inventory of Raw Materials	7,000		
Closing Inventory of Finished Goods	25,000		
Closing Inventory of Raw Materials	10,000		
Manufacturing Overheads	53,000		
COST OF GOODS SOLD			
MANUFACTURING COST			
Purchases of Raw Materials	50,000		
Opening Inventory of Work in Progress	8,000		
Opening Inventory of Finished Goods	30,000		
DIRECT COST			
DIRECT MATERIALS USED			
COST OF GOODS MANUFACTURED			

54 TETHYS LTD

Reorder the following costs into a manufacturing account format on the right side of the table below for the year ended 31 December. Enter the correct figures for the costs in bold that are not provided.

	£		£
DIRECT COST			
Direct Labour	15,000		
MANUFACTURING COST			
Opening Inventory of Raw Materials	5,000		
Closing Inventory of Finished Goods	16,000		
Purchases of Raw Materials	15,000		
DIRECT MATERIALS USED			
Manufacturing Overheads	25,000		
Closing Inventory of Raw Materials	8,000		
COST OF GOODS SOLD			
COST OF GOODS MANUFACTURED			
Opening Inventory of Finished Goods	12,000		
Opening Inventory of Work in Progress	4,000		
Closing Inventory of Work in Progress	6,000		

55   MULTI

Within a manufacturing account, the manufacturing costs are £45,000. Opening work in progress is £11,000, while opening finished goods were costed at £8,100. Closing work in progress is £9,700, while closing finished goods were £8,900.

What is Multi's cost of goods sold?

A   £44,500

B   £48,700

C   £45,500

D   £41,300

COSTING FOR INVENTORY AND WORK-IN-PROGRESS

NARRATIVE STYLE QUESTIONS

56   BOBBLE LTD

Match the disadvantage to the method of stock valuation by placing a tick in the relevant column of the table below.

Characteristic	FIFO	LIFO	AVCO
• Potentially out of date valuation on issues.			
• The valuation of inventory rarely reflects the actual purchase price of the material.			
• Potentially out of date closing inventory valuation.			

57   LINT LTD

Identify the following statements as either true or false by putting a tick in the relevant column of the table below.

Statement	True	False
• In periods of rising prices, FIFO gives a higher valuation of closing inventory than LIFO or AVCO.		
• In periods of falling prices, LIFO gives a higher valuation of issues of inventory than FIFO or AVCO.		
• AVCO would normally be expected to produce a valuation of closing inventory somewhere between valuations under FIFO and LIFO.		

58 FLUFF LTD

Identify the correct inventory valuation method from the characteristic given by putting a tick in the relevant column of the table below.

Characteristic	FIFO	LIFO	AVCO
• This inventory valuation method is particularly suited to inventory that consist of liquid materials e.g. oil.			
• This inventory valuation method is particularly suited to inventory that has a short shelf life e.g. dairy products.			
• This inventory valuation method is suited to a wheat farmer who has large silos of grain. Grain is added to and taken from the top of these silos.			

59 FIDO LTD

Identify the correct inventory valuation method from the characteristic given by putting a tick in the relevant column of the table below.

Characteristic	FIFO	LIFO	AVCO
• In times of rising prices this method will give higher profits.			
• In times of rising prices this method will give lower profits.			
• In times of rising prices this method gives a middle level of profits compared to the other two.			

60 TRUFFEAUX LTD

Identify whether the following statements are true or false by putting a tick in the relevant column of the table below.

Statement	True	False
• FIFO costs issues of inventory at the most recent purchase price.		
• AVCO costs issues of inventory at the oldest purchase price.		
• LIFO costs issues of inventory at the oldest purchase price.		
• FIFO values closing inventory at the most recent purchase price.		
• LIFO values closing inventory at the most recent purchase price.		
• AVCO values closing inventory at the latest purchase price.		

61   STOCKY LTD

Identify the correct inventory valuation method from the characteristic given by putting a tick in the relevant column of the table below.

Characteristic	FIFO	LIFO	AVCO
• Issues are valued at the most recent purchase cost.			
• Inventory is valued at the average of the cost of purchases.			
• Inventory is valued at the most recent purchase cost.			

INVENTORY CARDS

62   STONE LTD

Stone Ltd sells stone to builders. It had the following movements in one type of stone for the month of June:

DATE	RECEIPTS		ISSUES	
	Tonnes	Cost	Tonnes	Cost
June 1	500	£7,500		
June 8	350	£6,125		
June 15	275	£4,950		
June 22			650	
June 29	500	£8,750		

Complete the table below for the issue and closing inventory values, stating your answers to the nearest pound.

Method	Cost of Issue on 22 June	Closing Inventory at 30 June
FIFO	£	£
LIFO	£	£
AVCO	£	£

63   NATAL LTD

Natal Ltd makes and sells a wide range of clothes for babies. The following is an inventory card for Natal's most popular product for the month of December:

DATE	RECEIPTS		ISSUES	
	Units	Cost	Units	Cost
December 3	10,000	£85,000		
December 18	14,000	£112,000		
December 19	50,000	£350,000		
December 25			72,500	
December 29	5,000	£30,000		

Task 1

Complete the table below for the issue and closing inventory values. Give your answers to the nearest pound.

Method	Cost of Issue on 25 Dec	Closing Inventory at 29 Dec
LIFO	£	£
AVCO	£	£

Task 2

Identify the following statements as true or false by putting a tick in the relevant column of the table below.

	True	False
• FIFO would give a lower closing inventory valuation on the 29 December than LIFO and AVCO.		
• FIFO would give a lower cost of issue on the 25 December than LIFO and AVCO.		

64   GANDALF LTD

Gandalf Ltd has the following movements in a certain type of inventory into and out of its stores for the month of July.

DATE	RECEIPTS			ISSUES			BALANCE
	Units	Unit cost	Total £	Units	Unit cost	Total £	Total £
July 2	600	£1.50	£900				
July 4	500	£1.70	£850				
July 15				620			
July 19	200	£1.80	£360				
July 31				400			

Calculate the costs of the issues made on July 15 and July 31 if Gandalf plc uses a LIFO inventory valuation method.

	Valuation(£)
• July 15	
• July 31	

65   RIVALDO LTD

Rivaldo Ltd has the following movements in a certain type of inventory into and out of its stores for the month of April:

DATE	RECEIPTS		ISSUES	
	Units	Cost	Units	Cost
April 10	1000	£8,600		
April 23	600	£5,400		
April 26	500	£4,550		
April 29			600	
April 30	400	£3,640		

Complete the table below for the issue and closing inventory values.

Method	Cost of Issue on 29 April	Closing Inventory at 30 April
FIFO	£	£
LIFO	£	£
AVCO	£	£

66   SLOAN LTD

Sloan Ltd has the following movements in a certain type of inventory into and out of its stores for the month of March:

DATE	RECEIPTS		ISSUES	
	Units	Cost	Units	Cost
March 5	200	£600		
March 8	300	£1,200		
March 12	500	£2,500		
March 18			600	
March 25	400	£2,400		

Complete the table below for the issue and closing inventory values.

Method	Cost of Issue on 18 March	Closing Inventory at 25 March
FIFO	£	£
LIFO	£	£
AVCO	£	£

67 CRADBURY LTD

Cradbury Ltd has the following movements in a certain type of inventory into and out of it stores for the month of March:

DATE	RECEIPTS		ISSUES	
	Units	Cost	Units	Cost
March 1	100	£600		
March 2			30	
March 8	30	£195		
March 10			60	
March 15	100	£650		
March 16			40	

Task 1

Complete the table below for the issue and closing inventory values.

Method	Cost of Issue on 10 March	Closing Inventory at 16 March
FIFO	£	£
AVCO	£	£

Task 2

Identify the following statements as true or false by putting a tick in the relevant column of the table below.

	True	False
• LIFO would give a lower closing inventory valuation on the 16th March than FIFO and AVCO.		
• LIFO would give a lower cost of issue on the 10th March than FIFO and AVCO.		

68   EPIC LTD

You are told that the opening inventory of a single raw material in the stores is 8,000 units at £5 per unit. During the month, 12,000 units at £4.50 were received and the following week 14,000 units were issued.

Task 1

Identify the valuation method described in the statements below.

Characteristic	FIFO	LIFO	AVCO
• Closing inventory is valued at £28,200			
• The issue of inventory is valued at £67,000			
• The issue of inventory is valued at £64,000			

Task 2

Identify whether the statements in the table below are true or false by putting a tick in the relevant column.

	True	False
• AVCO values the issue of inventory at £65,800		
• LIFO values the closing inventory at £27,000		
• FIFO values the closing inventory at £30,000		

69   AWESOME LTD

You are told that the opening inventory of a single raw material in the stores is 6,000 units at £6 per unit. During the month, another 6,000 units at £10 were received and the following week 7,150 units were issued.

Task 1

Identify the valuation method described in the statements below.

Characteristic	FIFO	LIFO	AVCO
• Closing inventory is valued at £48,500			
• The issue of inventory is valued at £57,200			
• The issue of inventory is valued at £66,900			

Task 2

Identify whether the statements in the table below are true or false by putting a tick in the relevant column.

	True	False
• FIFO values the issue of inventory at £47,500.		
• AVCO values the closing inventory at £38,400		
• LIFO values the closing inventory at £29,100		

COSTING FOR LABOUR

NARRATIVE STYLE QUESTIONS

70 NULAB LTD

Identify the labour payment method by putting a tick in the relevant column of the table below.

Payment Method	Time- rate	Piecework	Piece-rate plus bonus
• Labour is paid based solely on the production achieved			
• Labour is paid extra if an agreed level of output is exceeded			
• Labour is paid according to hours worked			

71 LU LTD

Identify one advantage for each labour payment method by putting a tick in the relevant column of the table below.

Payment Method	Time- rate	Piecework	Time-rate plus bonus
• Assured level of remuneration for employee			
• Employee earns more if they work more efficiently than expected			
• Assured level of remuneration and reward for working efficiently			

72 MANDELA LTD

Identify whether the following statements are true or false in the relevant column of the table below.

Statement	True	False
• Time rate is paid based on the production achieved		
• Overtime is paid for hours worked over the standard hours agreed		
• Piece rate is paid according to hours worked		

73 PERRES LTD

Identify the hourly payment method by putting a tick in the relevant column of the table below.

Payment Method	Basic rate	Overtime premium	Overtime rate
• This is the amount paid above the basic rate for hours worked in excess of the normal hours			
• This is the total amount paid per hour for hours worked in excess of the normal hours			
• This is the amount paid per hour for normal hours worked			

74 TEVEZ LTD

Identify the following statements as true or false by putting a tick in the relevant column of the table below.

Statement	True	False
• Direct labour costs can be identified with the goods being made or the service being provided		
• Indirect labour costs vary directly with the level of activity		

75   BERDYCH LTD

Identify the whether the labour payment is usually associated with a fixed or variable cost by putting a tick in the relevant column of the table below.

Payment Method	Variable	Fixed
• Labour that is paid based on a time rate basis per hour worked		
• Labour is paid on a monthly salary basis		
• Labour that is based on number of units produced		

76   SODERLING LTD

Identify each labour payment method by putting a tick in the relevant column of the table below.

Payment Method	Time- rate	Piecework	Salary
• Assured level of remuneration for employee usually agreed for the year			
• Employee earnings are directly linked with units they produce			
• Employee earnings are directly linked with hours they work			

77   MURRAY LTD

Identify the following statements as true or false by putting a tick in the relevant column of the table below.

	True	False
• Indirect labour costs includes production supervisors' salaries		
• Direct labour costs usually vary directly with the level of activity		

78 OWEN LTD

Identify one advantage for each labour payment method by putting a tick in the relevant column of the table below.

Payment Method	Time- rate	Piecework	Salary
• Employee is paid the same amount every month			
• Employee wage increases in direct correlation with the number of hours worked			
• Employee wage increases in direct correlation with the number of units produced			

79 LABOUR STATEMENTS

Identify the following statements as either true or false by putting a tick in the relevant column of the table below.

Statement	True	False
• Piecework encourages employees to work harder		
• Piecework requires accurate recording of the number of hours staff have worked		
• Piecework encourages workers to improve the quality of the units they produce		

CALCULATING LABOUR COSTS

80 CONWAY LTD

Conway Ltd pays a time-rate of £6.50 per hour to its direct labour for a standard 35 hour week. Any of the labour force working in excess of 35 hours is paid an overtime rate of time and a half.

Calculate the gross wage for the week for the two workers in the table below.

Worker	Hours Worked	Basic Wage	Overtime	Gross Wage
J. Goldberg	35 hours	£	£	£
R. Spencer	40 hours	£	£	£

81 MIKEE LTD

Identify the following statements about the piecework method as either true or false by putting a tick in the relevant column of the table below.

Statement	True	False
Employees pay will rise if they work for more hours.		
An employee who is paid £210 for making 300 units is being paid 70p per unit.		
An employee will be penalized for poor quality production in a piecework system.		
An employee who is paid 65p for each unit made would earn £211.25 if they made 325 units.		

82 KAHN LTD

Kahn Ltd uses a time-rate method with bonus to pay its direct labour in one of its factories. The time-rate used is £12 per hour and a worker is expected to produce 5 units an hour, any time saved is paid at £6 per hour.

Calculate the gross wage for the week including bonus for the three workers in the table below.

Worker	Hours Worked	Units Produced	Basic Wage	Bonus	Gross Wage
A. Smith	35	175	£	£	£
J. O'Hara	35	180	£	£	£
M.Stizgt	35	185	£	£	£

83 STITCH LTD

Stitch Ltd pays a time-rate of £10 per hour to its direct labour force they are paid for a guaranteed standard 35 hour week. Any of the labour force working in excess of 35 hours is paid an overtime rate of £15 per hour.

Calculate the gross wage for the week for the three workers in the table below.

Worker	Hours Worked	Basic Wage	Overtime	Gross Wage
G. Brown	35 hours	£	£	£
N. Clegg	40 hours	£	£	£
D. Cameron	30 hours	£	£	£

84 PATTERSON LTD

Patterson Ltd uses a basic salary plus piecework method to pay labour in one of its factories. The basic salary is £180 per week the piece rate used is 10p per unit produced.

Calculate the gross wage for the week for the two workers in the table below.

Worker	Units Produced in Week	Gross Wage
Ahmad	300 units	£
G. Jones	400 units	£

85 NAILS R US LTD

Nails r us Ltd uses a time-rate method with bonus to pay its direct labour in one of its factories. The time-rate used is £15 per hour and a worker is expected to produce 10 units an hour, anything over this and the worker is paid a bonus of £2 per unit.

Calculate the gross wage for the week including bonus for the three workers in the table below.

Worker	Hours Worked	Units Produced	Basic Wage	Bonus	Gross Wage
M. Anchester	35	320	£	£	£
L. Ondon	35	370	£	£	£
L. Eeds	35	350	£	£	£

86 HOCKEY LTD

Hockey Ltd pays a time-rate of £15 per hour to its direct labour force a standard 35 hour week. Any of the labour force working in excess of 35 hours is paid an overtime rate of time and a quarter.

Calculate the gross wage for the **4-week** period for the three workers in the table below.

Worker	Hours Worked	Basic Wage	Overtime	Gross Wage
A. Smith	158	£	£	£
S. Patel	140	£	£	£
R. Cullen	160	£	£	£

87 DRACO LTD

Draco Ltd uses a piecework method to pay labour in one of its factories. The rate used is 80p per unit produced up to the standard number of units to be produced per week of 250. For any units over that the workers will get £10 per 20 units.

Calculate the gross wage for the week for the three workers in the table below.

Worker	Units Produced in Week	Gross Wage
P. Jones	240 units	£
D. Bannatyne	350 units	£
L. Redford	250 units	£

88   QUAGGA PLC

Quagga plc pays its employees £4.50 per hour and expects them to make 50 units per hour. Any excess production will be paid a bonus of 45p per unit.

Identify the following statements as being true or false by putting a tick in the relevant column of the table below.

Statement	True	False
During a 29 hour week, an employee producing 1,475 units would not receive a bonus.		
During a 32 hour week, an employee producing 1,665 units would receive a bonus of £29.25.		
During a 37 hour week, an employee producing 1,925 units would receive total pay of £300.25.		

89   SIRRIUS PLC

Sirrius plc uses a time-rate method with bonus to pay its direct labour in one of its factories. The time-rate used is £12 per hour and a worker is expected to produce 5 units an hour, anything over this and the worker is paid a bonus of £1 per unit.

Calculate the gross wage for a one week period including bonus for the three workers in the table below.

Worker	Hours Worked	Units Produced	Basic Wage	Bonus	Gross Wage
A. Carr	35	150	£	£	£
P. Kay	35	175	£	£	£
F. Boyle	35	210	£	£	£

90   DAVIDSON LTD

Davidson Ltd pays a basic wage of £150/week plus £0.10 per unit produced.

Calculate the gross wage for the week for the three workers in the table below.

Worker	Units produced	Basic Wage	Piece work	Gross Wage
P. Parker	350	£	£	£
C. Kent	315	£	£	£
M. Miles	280	£	£	£

91   GREENWOOD LTD

Greenwood Ltd pays a basic wage of £350/week equivalent to a time-rate of £10 per hour and a standard 35 hour week. Workers are expected to produce 5 units an hour and for units produced in excess of this a bonus is paid based on £7 for every hour saved.

So, for example, if 10 additional units are produced, then this would be equivalent to two hours saved and a bonus of £14 awarded.

Calculate the gross wage for the week including bonus for the three workers in the table below.

Worker	Hours Worked	Units Produced	Basic Wage	Bonus	Gross Wage
B. Ryan	35	175	£	£	£
S. Chang	35	190	£	£	£
E. Schneider	35	210	£	£	£

SPREADSHEETS AND VARIANCES

92   VARIOUS LTD

Identify the following statements as being true or false by putting a tick in the relevant column of the table below.

Statement	True	False
• A variance is the difference between budgeted and actual cost.		
• A favourable variance means actual costs are less than budgeted.		
• An adverse variance means that actual income is less than budgeted.		
• A spreadsheet can be used to store large amounts of financial information.		

93 SPREADSHEETS

Identify the following statements about spreadsheets as being true or false by putting a tick in the relevant column of the table below.

Statement	True	False
• Cells are used to enter data into a spreadsheet.		
• Spreadsheets cannot be protected, meaning that the data they contain is open for anyone to see.		
• The 'worksheet' refers to the entire spreadsheet file.		
• The 'sum' function is the only formula that can be used to sum a number of figures in a spreadsheet.		

94 STUFF LTD

Identify the following statements about spreadsheets as being true or false by putting a tick in the relevant column of the table below.

Statement	True	False
• Information can be entered into a spreadsheet either through typing it into the active cell or by entering it into the formula bar.		
• All formulas have to start with an equals sign (=) to be recognized by the spreadsheet.		
• Spreadsheet functions are only designed to allow users to add, subtract, multiply and divide figures.		
• Spreadsheets will not allow the user to display the information they contain using graphs.		

95   CALCVAR LTD

Calcvar Ltd has produced a spreadsheet detailing budgeted and actual cost for last month.

Task 1

Calculate the amount of the variance for each cost type and then determine whether it is adverse or favourable (enter A or F).

	A	B	C	D	E
1	Cost Type	Budget £	Actual £	Variance £	Adverse or favourable (A or F)
2	Direct Materials	250,000	278,350		
3	Direct Labour	180,000	179,280		
4	Production Overheads	150,000	146,750		
5	Administration Overheads	90,000	91,385		
6	Selling and Distribution Overheads	90,000	94,568		

Task 2

Insert the formulas in the table below that you used for cells 2 to 6 of column D.

	D
1	Variance £
2	
3	
4	
5	
6	

96   GRENOLA LTD

The following spreadsheet for this month has been produced for Grenola Ltd. Any variance in excess of 10% of budget is deemed to be significant.

Task 1

Calculate the variance as a % of the budget and enter your answer into the table below to the nearest whole percentage. Indicate whether the variance is significant or not by entering S for significant and NS for not significant.

	A	B	C	D	E	F
1	Cost Type	Budget	Variance	Adverse/ Favourable	Variance as % of budget	Significant or Not Significant
2	Direct Materials	£39,000	£3,300	Adverse		
3	Direct Labour	£75,000	£8,000	Adverse		
4	Production Overheads	£69,000	£8,800	Favourable		
5	Administration Overheads	£53,000	£5,900	Adverse		
6	Sales	£410,000	£21,000	Favourable		

Task 2

Insert the formulas in the table below that you used for cells 2 to 6 of column D.

	D
1	Variance £
2	
3	
4	
5	
6	

97 WYEDALE LTD

Wyedale Ltd has produced a spreadsheet detailing budgeted and actual cost for last month.

Calculate the amount of the variance in £ and % for each cost type and then determine whether it is adverse or favourable by putting an A or F the relevant column of the table below. State your percentage to the nearest whole number.

	A	B	C	D	E	F
1	Cost Type	Budget £	Actual £	Variance £	Variance %	Adverse/ Favourable
2	Sales	27,000	29,775			
3	Direct Materials	7,400	8,510			
4	Direct Labour	7,200	7,920			
5	Production Overheads	5,500	5,390			
6	Administration Overheads	4,500	4,365			

98 NETWORK LTD

The following spreadsheet for this month has been produced for Network Ltd as summarised in the table below. Any variance in excess of 5% of budget is deemed to be significant and should be reported to the relevant manager for review and appropriate action.

Determine whether the variance for each figure adverse or favourable by putting an A or F into the relevant column of the table below. Put an S in column E if the variance is significant or an NS if the variance is not significant.

	A	B	C	D	E
1		Budget	Actual	Adverse or Favourable (A or F)	Significant or Not Significant (S or NS)
2	Sales	£375,000	£363,200		
3	Direct Materials	£120,000	£117,600		
4	Direct Labour	£100,000	£115,000		
5	Production Overheads	£85,000	£88,400		

99   IVAN LTD

Ivan Ltd has produced a spreadsheet detailing budgeted and actual cost for last month.

Task 1

Calculate the amount of the variance for each cost type and then determine whether it is adverse or favourable by putting an A or an F into the relevant column below.

	A	B	C	D	E
1	Cost Type	Budget £	Actual £	Variance £	Adverse or favourable (A or F)
2	Sales	544,750	547,450		
3	Direct materials	76,800	80,200		
4	Direct Labour	148,400	146,000		
5	Production Overheads	136,000	144,200		
6	Administration Overheads	105,000	109,800		

Task 2

Insert the formulas in the table below that you used for cells 2 to 6 of column D.

	D
1	Variance £
2	
3	
4	
5	
6	

100 BLUEBELL LTD

The following spreadsheet for this month has been produced for Bluebell Ltd as summarised in the table below.

Task 1

Calculate the variances in the spreadsheet below and indicate whether they are adverse or favourable by putting an A or F in the relevant column and calculate the variance as a % to the nearest whole number.

	A	B	C	D	E	F
1	Cost Type	Budget	Actual	Variance (£)	Adverse/ Favourable	%
2	Sales	£204,555	£197,455			
3	Direct Materials	£39,000	£42,300			
4	Direct Labour	£75,000	£83,000			
5	Production Overheads	£69,000	£64,800			
6	Administration Overheads	£53,000	£58,900			

Task 2

Insert the formulas in the table below that you used for cells 2 to 6 of column F.

	F
1	Variance £
2	
3	
4	
5	
6	

101 ELVES LTD

Elves Ltd has started the production of a spreadsheet that will enable it to calculate its profit for each month of the first four months of the year. There was no opening or closing inventories. The first month has been completed.

Units sold: January – 14,000

                February – 16,000

                March – 12,000

                April – 14,500

Variable costs   £0.95 per unit

Sales   £1.50 per unit

Fixed costs   £7,500 per month

	A	B	C	D	E
1		*Sales (£)*	*?*	*?*	*?*
2	January	21,000	7,500	13,300	200
3	February				
4	March				
5	April				
6	Total				

Task 1

Decide which of the following headings should be entered into each of the cells C1, D1 and E1: Profit/loss, variable costs, fixed costs.

Cell	*Heading*
C1	Fixed costs
D1	Variable costs
E1	Profit/loss

Task 2

Complete the table above by entering the correct figures into the above table for rows 3 to 6 inclusive. Insert any losses as negative numbers.

Task 3

Insert the formulas in the table below that you used for row 6 of columns B, C, D and E.

	A	B	C	D	E
6	Total				

102 HOBBIT PLC

Hobbit plc has started the production of a spreadsheet that will enable it to calculate its total labour cost for the four weeks of the last month. The first week has been completed.

Hours worked: January – 2,566

                       February – 3,876

                       March – 4,663

                       April – 3,445

Average hourly rate paid   £12 per hour

Hobbit pays staff a bonus of 10% of their total standard pay each week where hours worked are in excess of 3,800.

	A	B	C	D	E	F
1		Standard hours	Standard hourly rate paid (£)	Total standard pay	Bonus	Gross pay
2	Week 1	2,566	12	30,792	0	30,792
3	Week 2					
4	Week 3					
5	Week 4					

Task 1

Complete the above table by entering the correct figures into the above table for rows 2 to 5 inclusive. Work to the nearest whole £.

Task 2

Insert the formulas in the table below that you used for column D, rows 2 to 5 inclusive.

	D
1	Total standard pay
2	
3	
4	
5	

Section 2

ANSWERS TO PRACTICE QUESTIONS

COST CLASSIFICATION

FINANCIAL AND MANAGEMENT ACCOUNTING

1   FAMA

Characteristic	Financial Accounting	Management Accounting
• Have to be produced annually	✓	
• Analyses historic events to help produce forecasts		✓
• Is always produced using accounting standards	✓	
• Is produced on an ad hoc basis when required		✓

2   FINANCIAL AND MANAGEMENT

Characteristic	Financial Accounting	Management Accounting
• Must be presented as specified by the Companies Act and accounting standards	✓	
• Helps managers run the business on a day-to-day basis		✓
• Used as the basis for the calculation of the organisation's tax charge.	✓	
• Can include anything that managers feel is useful for the business		✓

3   MAFA

Characteristic	Management Accounting	Financial Accounting
• It is based on past events		✓
• Its purpose is to provide information for managers	✓	
• It is based on future events	✓	
• It complies with company law and accounting rules		✓

4   FEATURES

Feature	Financial Accounting	Management Accounting
• Analysis of profit by cost centre		✓
• Statement of profit or loss using format as dictated by accounting standards and company law	✓	
• Cash flow forecasts		✓
• Cost per unit calculation		✓

COST AND PROFIT CENTRES

5   JEREMY

	Cost centre	Profit centre
• Bakery	✓	
• Shop		✓
• Office	✓	

6   PRINT PLC

Department	Cost centre	Profit centre
• Binding		✓
• Shops		✓
• Marketing	✓	

7   HOOCH PLC

Department	Cost centre	Profit centre	Investment centre
• Hooch's manager has no responsibility for income or asset purchases and disposals.	✓		
• Hooch's manager is assessed on the profitability of their department, as well as how effectively they have controlled their assets.			✓
• Hooch's manager is responsible for income and expenditure of their department only.		✓	

CLASSIFYING COSTS BY ELEMENT (MATERIALS, LABOUR OR OVERHEADS)

8   VVV LTD

Cost	Direct Materials	Direct Labour	Overheads
• Paint used on the planes	✓		
• Depreciation of the machines used in the factory			✓
• Oil used on the machines in the factory			✓
• Salary of worker assembling the planes		✓	

9   TRIP LTD

Cost	Materials	Labour	Overheads
• Wages of the insurance clerks dealing with claims		✓	
• Rent of the office			✓
• Paper used to print off insurance policies	✓		
• Salary of the office manager			✓

10   BMI LTD

Cost	Materials	Labour	Overheads
• Personal trainer's wages		✓	
• Electricity cost			✓
• Depreciation of gym equipment			✓
• Salary of the gym manager			✓

Note: you may feel that this question is badly designed as the salary of the gym manager is both a type of labour and an indirect cost (overhead). However, this question is based on one that appeared in the AAT sample assessment, where the "correct" answer was as given here. If you encounter such a question in your live assessment then hopefully it will not be unclear, but if it is, then adopt the approach here.

11   ACC LTD

Cost	Materials	Labour	Overheads
• Wages of the accountants		✓	
• Office water rates			✓
• Depreciation of the computers used by the accountants			✓
• Paper used by the accountants in their audits	✓		

CLASSIFYING COSTS BY NATURE (DIRECT OR INDIRECT)

12   LOVELOX LTD

Cost	Direct	Indirect
• Shampoo used on hair	✓	
• Depreciation of salons		✓
• Wages of salon cleaner		✓
• Wages of hair stylists	✓	

13   RUSSETT LTD

Cost	Direct	Indirect
• Glass used to make tablets	✓	
• Insurance of factory		✓
• Wages of workers assembling tablets	✓	
• Cost of entertaining corporate clients		✓

14 SCOTLAND LTD

Cost	Direct	Indirect
• Cleaners wages		✓
• Advertising expense		✓
• Material used in production	✓	
• Production managers wages		✓
• Machinist wages	✓	

15 DIRECT OR INDIRECT

Cost	Direct	Indirect
• Chargeable hour for a lawyer	✓	
• Machine hire for a building contractor in a long term contract	✓	
• Electricity for a garden centre		✓
• Audit fee for a restaurant		✓

16 DIRECT COSTS

B

Direct costs are variable and are therefore usually assumed to be constant, regardless of the level of activity within the relevant range. Answer A is incorrect because it describes the behaviour of a fixed cost within the relevant range of activity. Answer C also describes a fixed cost, since the same total fixed cost would be shared over a varying number of units, resulting in a unit cost that varies with changes in activity levels. Answer D is incorrect because total variable costs are conventionally deemed to remain unaltered when activity levels remain constant.

CLASSIFYING COSTS BY FUNCTION (PRODUCTION, ADMINISTRATION OR SELLING AND DISTRIBUTION

17 NOOGLE LTD

Cost	Production	Administration	Selling and distribution
• Purchases of plastic for ready meal containers	✓		
• Depreciation of sales department's delivery lorries			✓
• Insurance of office computers		✓	
• Salaries of production workers	✓		

18 HEAVING LTD

Cost	Production	Administration	Selling and distribution
• Paper used to print off sales invoices		✓	
• Metal used to make weights and bars	✓		
• Depreciation of sales person's vehicle			✓
• Repairs to machine in factory	✓		

19 KORMA PLC

Cost	Production	Administration	Selling and distribution	Finance
• Direct materials	✓			
• Sales director's salary			✓	
• Head office printer ink		✓		
• Direct labour	✓			
• Bank charges				✓

20 GREOGRIAN LTD

Cost	Production – direct costs	Production – overheads	Selling overheads
• Direct labour	✓		
• Power used in production machinery		✓	
• Training costs for new employees in advertising			✓
• Insurance for sales team cars			✓
• Insurance for production machinery		✓	

CLASSIFYING COSTS BY BEHAVIOUR (FIXED, VARIABLE OR SEMI-VARIABLE)

21   QUARK LTD

Cost	Fixed	Variable	Semi-variable
• Bar manager's salary	✓		
• Alcohol used to make drinks		✓	
• Rent of bar	✓		
• Telephone costs, including standard line rental charge			✓

22   MORN LTD

Cost	Fixed	Variable	Semi-variable
• Wood used in production		✓	
• Advertising manager's salary	✓		
• Electricity costs which include a standing charge			✓
• Labour costs paid on a piecework basis		✓	

23   STEPPED FIXED COST

A

A supervisor's wages are usually classified as a step cost because a supervisor may be responsible for supervising up to a specific number of workers. However, if output increases such that additional direct labour is required, then an extra supervisor will be required.

1 – 10 workers	1 supervisor
11 – 20 workers	2 supervisors

24   BRAETAK LTD

Cost	Fixed	Variable	Semi-variable
• Rent	✓		
• Wages of production workers paid on an hourly basis		✓	
• Wages of production workers paid by a piece rate method		✓	
• Sales staff paid a basic wage plus commission for each unit sold			✓

Note: the piece rate scheme does not mention a guaranteed minimum wage so the correct answer is variable.

25   ODO LTD

Cost	Fixed	Variable	Semi-variable
• Material used in the production process		✓	
• Safety review fee for the year	✓		
• Electricity costs which include a standing charge			✓
• Labour paid on a per unit basis		✓	

26   DEFINITIONS

Behaviour	Fixed	Variable	Semi-variable	Stepped cost
• This type of cost increases in direct proportion to the amount of units produced		✓		
• This type of cost has a fixed and a variable element			✓	
• This type of cost remains constant despite changes in output	✓			
• This type of cost is fixed within a certain range of output				✓

27   COSTS

   (a)   Variable cost per unit – graph 1

   (b)   Total fixed cost – graph 1

   (c)   Stepped fixed costs – graph 3

   (d)   Total variable cost – graph 2

   (e)   Semi-variable cost – graph 4

COST CODING

28   BYTES LTD

Cost	Code
• Salary of trainee IT consultant	• B100
• Planning costs to renew lease of the office	• C200
• Wages of the office manager	• B200
• Cleaning materials used by cleaner	• A200

29   SIMPLYFLY LTD

Transaction	Code
• Office heating	• 300/200
• Oil for the machines in production	• 200/200
• Sale to New York (US)	• 100/100
• Sale to Germany	• 100/200
• Fabric for seat covers	• 200/100
• Factory canteen wages	• 200/200

30   BUNTON LTD

Transaction	Code
• Petrol for lorries	• 400/200
• Warehouse rent	• 400/200
• Sales of water	• 100/100
• Rent received	• 100/200
• Materials to make plastic bottles	• 200/100

Note: As with a similar question in an AAT sample assessment, we are not told if the warehouse is for materials or finished goods. Assume the latter to get the "right" answer.

31   NAYULZ LTD

Cost	Code
• Salary of trainee nail technician	• B100
• Legal costs against a customer who refused to pay	• C200
• Wages of salon cleaner	• B200
• Heat and light for salon	• C200
• Nail polish used on customers	• A100

Note: do not let the question put you off – you cannot have direct overheads.

32   INDIANA LTD

Location	Code
• Whitewell High School (Kiveton)	• 100/200
• White Swan Hotel (Kiveton)	• 100/210
• Worcester Royal Hospital (Birmingham)	• 120/220
• Dudley Council Offices (Birmingham)	• 120/230
• Browns Hotel (Birmingham)	• 120/210
• Dunn and Musgrove Offices (Whitby)	• 110/230

33   GREENFINGERS

Cost	Code
• Purchase of seeds used to grow plants for resale	• A100
• Accountancy fees for preparation of year end accounts	• C200
• Wages of gardeners who maintain the plants to be sold	• B100
• Cleaning materials used by cleaner	• A200
• Salary of office manager	• B200

COST BEHAVIOUR

NARRATIVE STYLE QUESTIONS

34 BUNGLE LTD

Statement	True	False
• Total variable costs will decrease		✓
• Total fixed costs will remain the same	✓	
• The variable cost per unit will remain the same	✓	
• The fixed cost per unit will increase		✓

35 TF

Statement	True	False
• Variable costs change directly with changes in activity	✓	
• Fixed costs change directly with changes in activity		✓
• Stepped costs are fixed within a set range of output	✓	

36 FIXED OR VARIABLE

Cost	Fixed	Variable
• Direct materials		✓
• Power used in production machinery		✓
• Training costs for new employees in production	✓	
• Insurance for sales cars	✓	
• Insurance machinery	✓	
• Sales commission		✓

CALCULATION QUESTIONS

37   MARIO PLC

Statement	Fixed	Variable	Semi-variable
• Costs are £75,000, which is made up of a fixed charge of £45,000 and a further cost of £3 per unit at 7,000 units.			✓
• Costs are £75 per unit when 1,000 units are made and £15 per unit when 5,000 units are made.	✓		
• Costs are £65 per unit regardless of the number of units made.		✓	

38   TRIGEORGIS PLC

Statement	Fixed	Variable	Semi-variable
• Costs are £50,000 in total regardless of the number of units made.	✓		
• Costs are £50,000 in total when 2,500 units are made and £80,000 when 4,000 units are made.		✓	
• Costs are £7 per unit when 1,000 units are made and £6 per unit when 2,000 units are made.			✓

Note: The third cost must be semi-variable as it cannot be fixed (it changes as the number of units changes) and it cannot be purely variable as the cost per unit changes at different levels of activity.

39 JEEPERS LTD

Cost	Yes	No
• Materials used in production	✓	
• Piecework labour costs	✓	
• Salary of chief executive		✓

Element	Unit Product Cost
Materials	£35
Labour	£8
Direct cost	£43
Overheads	£38
Total	£81

40 TWO-PART PLC

Units	Fixed Costs	Variable Costs	Total Costs	Unit Cost
1,500	£15,000	£6,000	£21,000	£14
2,000	£15,000	£8,000	£23,000	£11.50
2,500	£15,000	£10,000	£25,000	£10
3,000	£15,000	£12,000	£27,000	£9

Statement	True	False
• The cost per unit increases as output increases due to the total variable costs increasing.		✓
• The cost per unit does not alter as output increases because the total cost increases.		✓
• The cost per unit decreases as output increases because the fixed costs are spread over more units.	✓	

41 GLORIA LTD

Element	Unit cost	Total Cost for 20,000 units
Variable production costs	£5.50	£110,000
Fixed production costs	£4.00	£80,000
Total production cost	£9.50	£190,000

42   METRIC LTD

Element	Unit Cost	Total cost
Materials	£5.00	£120,000
Labour	£12.00	£288,000
Overheads	£2.00	£48,000
Total	£19.00	£456,000

43   VINNY LTD

Element	Unit cost	Total cost
Materials	£5.00	£100,000
Labour	£8.00	£160,000
Overheads	£5.00	£100,000
Total	£18.00	£360,000

44   GREEGY LTD

Element	Unit Cost
Materials	£5.00
Labour	£1.50
Overheads	£2.00
Total	£8.50

45   SIMON LTD

Element	Total Cost for 20,000 units	Unit Cost
Direct costs	£140,000	£7.00
Production overhead	£80,000	£4.00
Non production overhead	£110,000	£5.50
Total costs	£330,000	£16.50

46   OLSEN LTD

Element	Total Cost	Unit cost
Materials	£960,000	£12.00
Labour	£1,360,000	£17.00
Production Overheads	£80,000	£1.00
Administration Overheads	£40,000	£0.50
Total	£2,440,000	£30.50

47 FLAKEWAY LTD

Element	Unit Cost
Materials	£5.00
Labour	£4.00
Overheads	£2.00
Total	£11.00

48 CORONATION LTD

	Total Cost for 5,000 units	Unit Cost
Direct costs	£32,500	£6.50
Production overhead	£40,000	£8.00
Non production overhead	£45,000	£9.00
Total costs	£117,500	£23.50

49 IRONSIDE LTD

Element	Unit Cost	Total cost
Materials	£30.00	£1,350,000
Labour	£12.00	£540,000
Overheads	£2.60	£117,000
Total	£44.60	£2,007,000

MANUFACTURING ACCOUNTS

50 MANU LTD

Manufacturing Account – Y/E 31 December

	£
Opening Inventory of Raw Materials	50,000
Purchases of Raw Materials	120,000
Closing Inventory of Raw Materials	65,000
DIRECT MATERIALS USED	105,000
Direct Labour	140,000
DIRECT COST	245,000
Manufacturing Overheads	85,000
MANUFACTURING COST	330,000
Opening Inventory of Work in Progress	48,000
Closing Inventory of Work in Progress	52,000
COST OF GOODS MANUFACTURED	326,000
Opening Inventory of Finished Goods	57,000
Closing Inventory of Finished Goods	61,000
COST OF GOODS SOLD	322,000

51 CHARTERIS LTD

Manufacturing Account – Y/E 31 July

	£
Opening Inventory of Raw Materials	10,000
Purchases of Raw Materials	60,000
Closing Inventory of Raw Materials	12,000
DIRECT MATERIALS USED	58,000
Direct Labour	88,000
DIRECT COST	146,000
Manufacturing Overheads	45,000
MANUFACTURING COST	191,000
Opening Inventory of Work in Progress	12,000
Closing Inventory of Work in Progress	15,000
FACTORY COST OF GOODS MANUFACTURED	188,000
Opening Inventory of Finished Goods	18,000
Closing Inventory of Finished Goods	20,000
COST OF GOODS SOLD	186,000

52 KRATOS LTD

Manufacturing Account – Y/E 31 May

	£
Opening Inventory of Raw Materials	14,000
Purchases of Raw Materials	100,000
Closing Inventory of Raw Materials	20,000
DIRECT MATERIALS USED	**94,000**
Direct Labour	194,000
DIRECT COST	**288,000**
Manufacturing Overheads	106,000
MANUFACTURING COST	**394,000**
Opening Inventory of Work in Progress	16,000
Closing Inventory of Work in Progress	20,000
COST OF GOODS MANUFACTURED	**390,000**
Opening Inventory of Finished Goods	60,000
Closing Inventory of Finished Goods	50,000
COST OF GOODS SOLD	**400,000**

53   SVEN LTD

Manufacturing Account – Y/E 31 May

	£
Opening Inventory of Raw Materials	7,000
Purchases of Raw Materials	50,000
Closing Inventory of Raw Materials	10,000
DIRECT MATERIALS USED	**47,000**
Direct Labour	97,000
DIRECT COST	**144,000**
Manufacturing Overheads	53,000
MANUFACTURING COST	**197,000**
Opening Inventory of Work in Progress	8,000
Closing Inventory of Work in Progress	10,000
COST OF GOODS MANUFACTURED	**195,000**
Opening Inventory of Finished Goods	30,000
Closing Inventory of Finished Goods	25,000
COST OF GOODS SOLD	**200,000**

54   TETHYS LTD

Manufacturing Account – Y/E 31 December

	£
Opening Inventory of Raw Materials	5,000
Purchases of Raw Materials	15,000
Closing Inventory of Raw Materials	8,000
DIRECT MATERIALS USED	**12,000**
Direct Labour	15,000
DIRECT COST	**27,000**
Manufacturing Overheads	25,000
MANUFACTURING COST	**52,000**
Opening Inventory of Work in Progress	4,000
Closing Inventory of Work in Progress	(6,000)
COST OF GOODS MANUFACTURED	**50,000**
Opening Inventory of Finished Goods	12,000
Closing Inventory of Finished Goods	(16,000)
COST OF GOODS SOLD	**46,000**

55   MULTI

C – Manufacturing cost + opening WIP – closing WIP + opening FG – closing FG

COSTING FOR INVENTORY AND WORK-IN-PROGRESS

NARRATIVE STYLE QUESTIONS

56   BOBBLE LTD

Characteristic	FIFO	LIFO	AVCO
• Potentially out of date valuation of inventory issues	✓		
• The valuation of inventory rarely reflects the actual purchase price of the material			✓
• Potentially out of date closing inventory valuation		✓	

57   LINT LTD

Statement	True	False
• In periods of rising prices, FIFO gives a higher valuation of closing inventory than LIFO or AVCO.	✓	
• In periods of falling prices, LIFO gives a higher valuation of issues of inventory than FIFO or AVCO.		✓
• AVCO would normally be expected to produce a valuation of closing inventory somewhere between valuations under FIFO and LIFO.	✓	

58   FLUFF LTD

Characteristic	FIFO	LIFO	AVCO
• This inventory valuation method is particularly suited to inventory that consist of liquid materials e.g. oil.			✓
• This inventory valuation method is suited to inventory that has a short shelf life e.g. dairy products.	✓		
• This inventory valuation method is suited to a wheat farmer who has large silos of grain. Grain is added to and taken from the top of these silos.		✓	

59 FIDO LTD

Characteristic	FIFO	LIFO	AVCO
• In times of rising prices this method will give higher profits.	✓		
• In times of rising prices this method will give lower profits		✓	
• In times of rising prices this method gives a middle level of profits compared to the other two.			✓

60 TRUFFEAUX LTD

Statement	True	False
• FIFO costs issues of inventory at the most recent purchase price.		✓
• AVCO costs issues of inventory at the oldest purchase price.		✓
• LIFO costs issues of inventory at the oldest purchase price.		✓
• FIFO values closing inventory at the most recent purchase price.	✓	
• LIFO values closing inventory at the most recent purchase price.		✓
• AVCO values closing inventory at the latest purchase price.		✓

61 STOCKY LTD

Characteristic	FIFO	LIFO	AVCO
• Issues are valued at the most recent purchase cost.		✓	
• Inventory is valued at the average of the cost of purchases.			✓
• Inventory is valued at the most recent purchase cost.	✓		

INVENTORY CARDS

62 STONE LTD

Method	Cost of Issue on 22 June	Closing Inventory at 30 June
FIFO	£10,125 (500 × £15) + (150 × £17.50)	£17,200 (£8,750 + £4,950 + £6,125 + £7,500) − £10,125
LIFO	£11,450 (275 × £18) + (350 x £17.50) + (25 × £15)	£15,875 (£8,750 + £4,950 + £6,125 + £7,500) − £11,450
AVCO	£10,732 ((£7,500 + £6,125 + £4,950)/(500 + 350 + 275)) × 650	£16,593 (£8,750 + £4,950 + £6,125 + £7,500) − £10,732

63   NATAL LTD

Task 1

Method	Cost of Issue on 2ʰ Dec	Closing Inventory at 29 Dec
LIFO	£534,250 **(50,000 × £7) + (14,000 × £8) + (8500 × £8.50)**	£42,750 **(£85,000 + £112,000 + £350,000 + £30,000) − £534,250**
AVCO	£535,912 **((£85,000 + £112,000 + £350,000)/(10,000 + 14,000 + 50,000)) × 72,500**	£41,088 **(£85,000 + £112,000 + £350,000 + £30,000) − £535,912**

Task 2

	True	False
• FIFO would give a lower closing inventory valuation on the 29ᵗʰ December than LIFO and AVCO	✓	
• FIFO would give a lower cost of issue on the 25ᵗʰ of December than LIFO and AVCO		✓

64   GANDALF LTD

	Valuation(£)
• July 15	£1,030 **(500 × £1.70) + (120 × £1.50)**
• July 31	£660 **(200 × £1.80) + (200 × £1.50)**

65   RIVALDO LTD

Method	Cost of Issue on 29 April	Closing Inventory at 30 April (Note)
FIFO	£5,160 (600 × £8.60)	£17,030
LIFO	£5,450 (100 × £9 + 500 × £9.10)	£16,740
AVCO	£5,303 (AVCO = £18,560/2,100 = £8.8381 Cost of issue = 600 × £8.8381)	£16,880

Tutorial note

The quickest way to calculate closing inventory is as total purchases (£22,190) less cost of issues.

66   SLOAN LTD

Method	Cost of Issue on 18 March	Closing Inventory at 25 March (Note)
FIFO	£2,300 (200 × £3 + 300 × £4 +100 × £5)	£4,400
LIFO	£2,900 (100 × £4 +500 × £5)	£3,800
AVCO	£2,580 (AVCO = 4,300/1,000 = £4.30/unit, giving cost of issue of 600 × £4.30)	£4,120

Tutorial note

Quickest to calculate closing inventory as total purchases (£6,700) less cost of issue

67   CRADBURY LTD

Tutorial note

This question is harder than those seen in the sample assessment but is here to give you more of a challenge!

Task 1

Method	Cost of Issue on 10 March	Closing Inventory at 16 March
FIFO	£360 (Note 1)	£650 (Note 2)
AVCO	£369 (Note 3)	£640 (Note 4)

Note 1:   All issues made from inventory bought on 1 March @ £6/unit

Note 2:   Closing inventory = just the March 15 purchases

Note 3:   AVCO per unit at March 10 = (70 × £6 + £195)/100 = £615/100 = £6.15/unit

Cost of issue thus = 60 × £6.15 = £369

Note 4:   AVCO per unit at March 16 = (40 × £6.15 + £650)/140 = £896/140 = £6.40/unit

Closing inventory thus = 100 × £6.40= £640

Task 2

	True	False
• LIFO would give a lower closing inventory valuation on the 16 March than FIFO and AVCO	✓	
• LIFO would give a lower cost of issue on the 10 March than FIFO and AVCO		✓

Tutorial note

If you spotted that we have a situation of rising prices then the comments about LIFO are easier.

68 EPIC LTD

Task 1

Characteristic	FIFO	LIFO	AVCO
• Closing inventory is valued at £28,200			✓
• The issue of inventory is valued at £67,000	✓		
• The issue of inventory is valued at £64,000		✓	

Task 2

	True	False
• AVCO values the issue of inventory at £65,800	✓	
• LIFO values the closing inventory at £27,000		✓
• FIFO values the closing inventory at £30,000		✓

69 AWESOME LTD

Task 1

Characteristic	FIFO	LIFO	AVCO
• Closing inventory is valued at £48,500	✓		
• The issue of inventory is valued at £57,200			✓
• The issue of inventory is valued at £66,900		✓	

Task 2

	True	False
• FIFO values the issue of inventory at £47,500.	✓	
• AVCO values the closing inventory at £38,400		✓
• LIFO values the closing inventory at £29,100	✓	

COSTING FOR LABOUR

NARRATIVE STYLE QUESTIONS

70   NULAB LTD

Payment Method	Time- rate	Piecework	Piece-rate plus bonus
• Labour is paid based on the production achieved		✓	
• Labour is paid extra if an agreed level of output is exceeded			✓
• Labour is paid according to hours worked	✓		

71   LU LTD

Payment Method	Time- rate	Piecework	Time-rate plus bonus
• Assured level of remuneration for employee	✓		
• Employee earns more if they work more efficiently than expected		✓	
• Assured level of remuneration and reward for working efficiently			✓

72   MANDELA LTD

Statement	True	False
• Time rate is paid based on the production achieved.		✓
• Overtime is paid for hours worked over the standard hours agreed.	✓	
• Piece rate is paid according to hours worked.		✓

73 PERRES LTD

Payment Method	Basic rate	Overtime premium	Overtime rate
• This is the amount paid above the basic rate for hours worked in excess of the normal hours.		✓	
• This is the total amount paid per hour for hours worked in excess of the normal hours.			✓
• This is the amount paid per hour for normal hours worked.	✓		

74 TEVEZ LTD

Statement	True	False
• Direct labour costs can be identified with the goods being made or the service being provided.	✓	
• Indirect labour costs vary directly with the level of activity.		✓

75 BERDYCH LTD

Payment Method	Variable	Fixed
• Labour that is paid based on a time rate basis per hour worked.	✓	
• Labour is paid on a monthly salary basis.		✓
• Labour that is based on number of units produced.	✓	

76 SODERLING LTD

Payment Method	Time- rate	Piecework	Salary
• Assured level of remuneration for employee usually agreed for the year			✓
• Employee earnings are directly linked with units they produce		✓	
• Employee earnings are directly linked with hours they work	✓		

77   MURRAY LTD

	True	False
• Indirect labour costs includes production supervisors' salaries	✓	
• Direct labour costs usually vary directly with the level of activity	✓	

78   OWEN LTD

Payment Method	Time-rate	Piecework	Salary
• Employee is paid the same amount every month			✓
• Employee wage increases in direct correlation with the number of hours worked	✓		
• Employee wage increases in direct correlation with the number of units produced		✓	

79   LABOUR STATEMENTS

Statement	True	False
• Piecework encourages employees to work harder	✓	
• Piecework requires accurate recording of the number of hours staff have worked		✓
• Piecework encourages workers to improve the quality of the units they produce		✓

CALCULATING LABOUR COSTS

80   CONWAY LTD

Worker	Hours Worked	Basic Wage	Overtime	Gross Wage
J. Goldberg	35 hours	£227.50	£0	£227.50
R. Spencer	40 hours	£227.50	£48.75	£276.25

81   MIKEE LTD

Statement	True	False
Employees pay will rise if they work for more hours.		✓
An employee who is paid £210 for making 300 units is being paid 70p per unit.	✓	
An employee will be penalized for poor quality production in a piecework system.		✓
An employee who is paid 65p for each unit made would earn £211.25 if they made 325 units.	✓	

82   KAHN LTD

Worker	Hours Worked	Units Produced	Basic Wage	Bonus	Gross Wage
A. Smith	35	175	£420	£0	£420
J. O'Hara	35	180	£420	£6	£426
M.Stizgt	35	185	£420	£12	£432

83   STITCH LTD

Worker	Hours Worked	Basic Wage	Overtime	Gross Wage
G. Brown	35 hours	£350	£0	£350
N. Clegg	40 hours	£350	£75	£425
D. Cameron	30 hours	£350	£0	£350

84   PATTERSON LTD

Worker	Units Produced in Week	Gross Wage
Ahmad	300 units	£210
G. Jones	400 units	£220

85   NAILS R US LTD

Worker	Hours Worked	Units Produced	Basic Wage	Bonus	Gross Wage
M. Anchester	35	320	£525	£0	£525
L. Ondon	35	370	£525	£40	£565
L. Eeds	35	350	£525	£0	£525

86 HOCKEY LTD

Worker	Hours Worked	Basic Wage	Overtime	Gross Wage
A. Smith	158	£2,100	£337.50	£2,437.50
S. Patel	140	£2,100	–	£2,100.00
R. Cullen	160	£2,100	£375.00	£2475.00

87 DRACO LTD

Worker	Units Produced in Week	Gross Wage
P. Jones	240 units	£192
D. Bannatyne	350 units	£250
L. Redford	250 units	£200

88 QUAGGA PLC

Statement	True	False
During a 29 hour week, an employee producing 1,475 units would not receive a bonus.		✓
During a 32 hour week, an employee producing 1,665 units would receive a bonus of £29.25.	✓	
During a 37 hour week, an employee producing 1,925 units would receive total pay of £300.25.		✓

89 SIRRIUS PLC

Worker	Hours Worked	Units Produced	Basic Wage	Bonus	Gross Wage
A. Carr	35	150	£420	£0	£420
P. Kay	35	175	£420	£0	£420
F. Boyle	35	210	£420	£35	£455

90 DAVIDSON LTD

Worker	Units produced	Basic Wage	Piece work	Gross Wage
P. Parker	350	£150	£35.00	£185.00
C. Kent	315	£150	£31.50	£181.50
M. Miles	280	£150	£28.00	£178.00

91   GREENWOOD LTD

Worker	Hours Worked	Units Produced	Basic Wage	Bonus	Gross Wage
B. Ryan	35	175	£350	£0	£350
S. Chang	35	190	£350	£21	£371
E. Schneider	35	210	£350	£49	£399

SPREADSHEETS AND VARIANCES

92   VARIOUS LTD

Statement	True	False
• A variance is the difference between budgeted and actual cost.	✓	
• A favourable variance means actual costs are less than budgeted.	✓	
• An adverse variance means that actual income is less than budgeted.	✓	
• A spreadsheet can be used to store large amounts of financial information.	✓	

93   SPREADSHEETS

Identify the following statements about spreadsheets as being true or false by putting a tick in the relevant column of the table below.

Statement	True	False
• Cells are used to enter data into a spreadsheet.	✓	
• Spreadsheets cannot be protected, meaning that the data they contain is open for anyone to see.		✓
• The 'worksheet' refers to the entire spreadsheet file.		✓
• The 'sum' function is the only formula that can be used to sum a number of figures in a spreadsheet.		✓

94 STUFF LTD

Identify the following statements about spreadsheets as being true or false by putting a tick in the relevant column of the table below.

Statement	True	False
• Information can be entered into a spreadsheet either through typing it into the active cell or by entering it into the formula bar.	✓	
• All formulas have to start with an equals sign (=) to be recognized by the spreadsheet.	✓	
• Spreadsheet functions are only designed to allow users to add, subtract, multiply and divide figures.		✓
• Spreadsheets will not allow the user to display the information they contain using graphs.		✓

VARIANCE SPREADSHEET QUESTIONS

95 CALCVAR LTD

Task 1

	A	B	C	D	E
1	Cost Type	Budget £	Actual £	Variance £	Adverse or favourable (A or F)
2	Direct Materials	250,000	278,350	28,350	A
3	Direct Labour	180,000	179,280	720	F
4	Production Overheads	150,000	146,750	3,250	F
5	Administration Overheads	90,000	91,385	1,385	A
6	Selling and Distribution Overheads	90,000	94,568	4,568	A

Task 2

	D
1	Variance £
2	=(B2–C2)
3	=(B3–C3)
4	=(B4–C4)
5	=(B5–C5)
6	=(B6–C6)

96   GRENOLA LTD

Task 1

	A	B	C	D	E	F
1	Cost Type	Budget	Variance	Adverse/ Favourable	Variance as % of budget	Significant or Not Significant
2	Direct Materials	£39,000	£3,300	Adverse	8	NS
3	Direct Labour	£75,000	£8,000	Adverse	11	S
4	Production Overheads	£69,000	£8,800	Favourable	13	S
5	Administration Overheads	£53,000	£5,900	Adverse	11	S
6	Sales	£410,000	£21,000	Favourable	5	NS

Task 2

	D
1	Variance £
2	=C2/B2
3	=C3/B3
4	=C4/B4
5	=C5/B5
6	=C6/B6

97   WYEDALE LTD

	A	B	C	D	E	F
1	Cost Type	Budget £	Actual £	Variance £	Variance %	Adverse/ Favourable
2	Sales	27,000	29,775	2,775	10	F
3	Direct Materials	7,400	8,510	1,110	15	A
4	Direct Labour	7,200	7,920	720	10	A
5	Production Overheads	5,500	5,390	110	2	F
6	Administration Overheads	4,500	4,365	135	3	F

98   NETWORK LTD

	A	B	C	D	E
1		Budget	Actual	Adverse or Favourable	Significant or Not Significant
2	Sales	£375,000	£363,200	A	NS
3	Direct Materials	£120,000	£117,600	F	NS
4	Direct Labour	£100,000	£115,000	A	S
5	Production Overheads	£85,000	£88,400	A	NS

99   IVAN LTD

Task 1

	A	B	C	D	E
1	Cost Type	Budget £	Actual £	Variance £	Adverse or favourable (A or F)
2	Sales	544,750	547,450	2,700	F
3	Direct materials	76,800	80,200	3,400	A
4	Direct Labour	148,400	146,000	2,400	F
5	Production Overheads	136,000	144,200	8,200	A
6	Administration Overheads	105,000	109,800	4,800	A

Task 2

	D
1	Variance £
2	=B2–C2
3	=B3–C3
4	=B4–C4
5	=B5–C5
6	=B6–C6

100   BLUEBELL LTD

Task 1

	A	B	C	D	E	F
1	Cost Type	Budget	Actual	Variance (£)	Adverse/ Favourable	%
2	Sales	£204,555	£197,455	7,100	A	3
3	Direct Materials	£39,000	£42,300	3,300	A	8
4	Direct Labour	£75,000	£83,000	8,000	A	11
5	Production Overheads	£69,000	£64,800	4,200	F	6
6	Administration Overheads	£53,000	£58,900	5,900	A	11

Task 2

	F
1	Variance £
2	=D2/B2
3	=D3/B3
4	=D4/B4
5	=D5/B5
6	=D6/B6

101   ELVES LTD

Task 1

Cell	Heading
C1	Fixed costs
D1	Variable costs
E1	Profit/loss

Task 2

	A	B	C	D	E
1		Sales (£)	Fixed costs	Variable costs	Profit/loss
2	January	21,000	7,500	13,300	200
3	February	24,000	7,500	15,200	1,300
4	March	18,000	7,500	11,400	−900
5	April	21,750	7,500	13,775	475
6	Total	84,750	30,000	53,675	1,075

Task 3

	A	B	C	D	E
6	Total	=sum(B2:B5)	=sum(C2:C5)	=sum(D2:D5)	=sum(D2:D5) or =B6-C6-D6

Note: Other formulas would have been acceptable. For instance, the formula in cell B6 could have been '=B2+B3+B4+B5'.

102 HOBBIT PLC

Task 1

	A	B	C	D	E	F
1		Standard hours	Standard hourly rate paid (£)	Total standard pay	Bonus	Gross pay
2	Week 1	2,566	12	30,792	0	30,792
3	Week 2	3,876	12	46,512	4,651	51,163
4	Week 3	4,663	12	55,956	5,596	61,552
5	Week 4	3,445	12	41,340	0	41,340

Task 2

	D
1	Total standard pay
2	=B2*C2
3	=B3*C3
4	=B4*C4
5	=B5*C5

Section 3

MOCK EXAM QUESTIONS

TASK 1

(a) **Identify the following statements as being true or false by putting a tick in the relevant column of the table below.**

Statement	True	False
• Labour paid by a simple piecework system is a variable cost.		
• FIFO is a useful inventory valuation method for materials where individual units are not separately identifiable.		
• A cost unit is a separately identifiable part of the business where the manager is only responsible for divisional costs.		
• Classification of cost by behaviour is particularly useful for budgeting.		

(b) **Indicate whether each of the following statements regarding management accounting is true or false by putting a tick in the relevant column of the table below.**

Characteristic	True	False
• Statements produced by management accounting is primarily for internal use		
• Management accounting statements are typically used to help identify the organisation's tax liability.		
• Management accountants produce the statement of profit or loss (income statement).		
• Management accounting statements normally focus on analysing past transactions.		

TASK 2

Morden makes and sells postcards.

(a) **Classify the following costs by element (material, labour or overhead) by putting a tick in the relevant column of the table below.**

Cost	Material	Labour	Overheads
• Wages paid to Morden's photographer for pictures used in postcards.			
• Ink used to print postcards			
• Maintenance of printers used to produce postcards			
• Delivery costs to customers			

Mitcham buys large rolls of wire, cuts them into various sizes and sells it on to customers.

(b) **Classify the following costs by nature (direct or indirect) by putting a tick in the relevant column of the table below.**

Cost	Direct	Indirect
• Wages of cutting staff		
• Depreciation of cutting machinery		
• Wages of the cutting staff supervisor		
• Purchase of rolls of wire		

TASK 3

Bank is a company that builds houses.

(a) **Classify the following costs by function (production, admin, selling and distribution or finance) by putting a tick in the relevant column of the table below.**

Cost	Production	Admin	Selling and Distribution	Finance
• Bank charges				
• Purchase of bricks				
• Depreciation of office computers				
• Wages paid to advertising staff				

(b) **Classify the following costs by behaviour (fixed, variable, semi-variable or stepped) by putting a tick in the relevant column of the table below.**

Statement	Fixed	Variable	Semi-variable	Stepped
• Purchase of land to be used for building new houses				
• Hire of digging equipment. One digger is required for every 15 houses built.				
• Bank' total wages bill – including salaried workers as well as those paid piecework.				
• Rent on Bank's head office building.				

TASK 4

Cesto Plc is a supermarket and uses a coding system for its elements of cost (materials, labour or overheads) and then further classifies each element by nature (direct or indirect cost) as below. So, for example, the code for direct materials is A100.

Element of Cost	Code	Nature of Cost	Code
Materials	A	Direct	100
		Indirect	200
Labour	B	Direct	100
		Indirect	200
Overheads	C	Direct	100
		Indirect	200

Code the following costs, extracted from invoices and payroll, using the table below.

Cost	Code
• Purchase of milk for resale in Cesto's stores	
• Wages of shelf-stackers in Cesto's stores	
• Salaries of Cesto's store managers	
• Public indemnity insurance	
• Purchase of cleaning products for resale in Cesto's stores	
• Supermarket staff canteen wages	

TASK 5

FFF is a company that manufactures three different types of fizzy drink – A, B and C. It uses an alpha code for the revenue, costs or investments and then further classifies numerically as shown below.

Activity	Code	Nature of Cost	Sub-code
Revenues	RE	Drink A	100
		Drink B	200
		Drink C	300
Costs	CO	Material	520
		Labour	620
		Overheads	720
Investments	IV	Drink A	100
		Drink B	200
		Drink C	300

Code the following costs, extracted from invoices and payroll, using the table below. Each transaction should have a five character code.

Cost	Code
• Investment in new machinery to manufacture Drink A	
• Wages paid to staff making Drink C	
• Sales of Drink C to Cesto Supermarkets	
• Purchase of sugar for use in Drinks A and C	
• Head office rental	
• Investment in new factory for Drink C	

TASK 6

(a)   **Identify the type of cost behaviour (fixed, variable or stepped) described in each statement by putting a tick in the relevant column of the table below.**

Statement	Fixed	Variable	Stepped
• Costs are £2,000 at 3,000 to 4,000 units and £4,000 at 5,000 to 6,000 units.			
• Cost per unit is £5 per unit if 10,000 units are made and £10 per unit if 5,000 units are made.			
• Total cost is £10,000 if 2,500 units are made and £16,000 if 4,000 units are made.			

(b)   **Identify the type of cost behaviour (fixed, variable or stepped) described in each statement by putting a tick in the relevant column of the table below**

Cost	Fixed	Variable
• Salary of managing director		
• Annual cost of accounts preparation		
• Design royalty paid on every unit made		

TASK 7

(a)   **Identify the following costs are an overhead or not by putting a tick in the relevant column of the table below.**

Statement	Yes	No
• Depreciation of production machinery		
• Fees paid for an external health and safety audit of production		
• Hours paid to workers on a piecework basis		

Jericho Ltd makes a single product and for a production level of 16,000 units has the following cost details:

Materials   8,000 kilos at £5 per kilo

Labour   32,000 hours at £8 an hour

Fixed Overheads   £224,000

(b)   **Complete the table below to show the unit cost at a REVISED production level of 20,000 units. Work to the nearest penny.**

Element	Unit Cost
Materials	£
Labour	£
Overheads	£
Total	£

TASK 8

(a) Reorder the following costs into a manufacturing account format for the year ended 31 June. Use the columns to the right of the table below to enter your answer.

Purchases of raw materials	22,000		
Direct labour	45,000		
Opening inventory of finished goods	2,500		
COST OF GOODS SOLD			
Opening inventory of raw materials	6,000		
DIRECT MATERIALS USED			
Manufacturing overheads	17,000		
Opening inventory of work in progress	4,000		
Closing inventory of finished goods	4,500		
MANUFACTURING COST			
Closing inventory of work in progress	2,800		
Closing inventory of raw materials	6,400		
DIRECT COST			
COST OF GOODS MANUFACTURED			

(b) Enter the correct figures for the following costs which were not provided in part (a).

Cost	£
DIRECT MATERIALS USED	
DIRECT COST	
MANUFACTURING COST	
COST OF GOODS MANUFACTURED	
COST OF GOODS SOLD	

TASK 9

Gravy Ltd carries a single type of raw material. At the start of the month, there were 25,000 litres of the material in inventory, valued at £6 per litre. During the month, Gravy bought another 50,000 litres at £3.75 per litre, followed by an issue to production of 60,000 litres at £7 per litre.

(a) Identify the valuation method described in the statements below by putting a tick in the relevant column.

Statement	FIFO	LIFO	AVCO
Closing inventory is valued at £67,500.			
The issue of inventory is costed at £281,250.			
The issue of inventory is costed at £247,500.			

(b)   **Identify whether the statements in the table are true or false by putting a tick in the relevant column.**

Statement	True	False
• FIFO values closing inventory at £90,000.		
• LIFO values closing inventory at £56,250.		
• AVCO values the issue of inventory at £270,000.		

TASK 10

Boat Ltd has the following movements in a certain type of stock into and out of it stores for the month of July:

DATE	RECEIPTS		ISSUES	
	Units	Cost	Units	Cost
July 6	350	£6,125		
July 12	500	£8,125		
July 17	150	£2,850		
July 22			400	
July 30	100	£2,000		

Complete the table below for the issue and closing stock values. Enter figures to the nearest penny.

Method	Cost of Issue on July 22	Closing Stock at July 31
FIFO	£	£
LIFO	£	£
AVCO	£	£

TASK 11

An employee is paid £5 per unit, and is expected to make 3 units per hour. Any work in excess of this is paid a bonus of £0.50 per unit.

(a)   **Identify the following statements as either true or false by putting a tick in the relevant column of the table below.**

Statement	True	False
• During a 31 hour working week, the employee made 92 units and did not receive a bonus.		
• During a 34 hour working week, the employee made 107 units and earned total pay of £537.50.		
• During a 25 hour week, the employee made 74 units and earned a £0.50 bonus.		

Daft Ltd pays a time-rate of £15 per hour to its direct labour for a standard 35 hour week. Any of the labour force working in excess of 35 hours is paid an overtime rate of 'time and a half'.

(b)   **Calculate the gross wage for the week for the two workers in the table below.**

Worker	Hours Worked	Basic Wage	Overtime	Gross Wage
S. Illy	37 hours	£	£	£
C. Razy	43 hours	£	£	£

TASK 12

Identify the following statements regarding labour payments as either true or false by putting a tick in the relevant column.

Statement	True	False
• An employee who is paid piecework could see a rise in their total pay if they work more hours.		
• Fixed salary staff are likely to have a higher focus on quality than staff who are paid piecework.		
• Employees who are paid an hourly rate will earn more if they are more productive.		
• Piecework systems enable the company to cut its wages expense if it does not need to make any more units.		

TASK 13

Jerry is paid £6.00 per unit produced, with a guaranteed minimum of £78 per full day he works.

Complete the table for Jerry's pay for the week

Day	Units made	Pay £
Monday	10	
Tuesday	15	
Wednesday	18	
Thursday	9	
Friday	20	
Total weekly wage		

TASK 14

Gassy Ltd has started the production of a spreadsheet which will enable it to calculate its profits for each month of the previous quarter.

Gassy had the following information for the four months:

Units made and sold:	April – 700
	May – 600
	June – 650
	July – 490
Variable costs	£6.00 per unit
Sales	£7.50 per unit
Fixed costs	£760 per month

	A	B	C	D	E	F
1		?	Variable costs	?	?	Profit/(loss)
2	April	5,250	4,200	760	4,960	290
3	May					
4	June					
5	July					
6	Total					

(a)   **Decide which of the following headings should be entered into each of the cells B1, D1 and E1.**

Fixed costs

Sales

Total costs

Cell	Heading
B1	
D1	
E1	

(b)   **Complete the table shown previously by entering the correct figures into the empty cells for rows 3 to 6 inclusive. Enter losses as negative numbers (i.e. a loss of £100 should be entered as -100)**

(c) **Insert the formulas in the table below that you used for row 6 of columns B, C, D and F. (Note: column E is NOT required).**

	A	B	C	D	F
6	Total				

TASK 15

Statement	True	False
• Spreadsheet formulas should always start with an equals sign.		
• A worksheet refers to an individual page of the spreadsheet file.		
• The 'ascending' function in a spreadsheet will be labeled 'A→Z'.		
• Changing the order of lists of data is the only major function in a spreadsheet.		

TASK 16

Sharp Ltd has produced a performance report detailing budgeted and actual information for last month.

(a) **Calculate the amount of the variance for each cost type and enter it into the spreadsheet below. Determine whether it is adverse or favourable and put an A or F in column E.**

	A	B	C	D	E
1	Cost Type	Budget £	Actual £	Variance	Adverse or Favourable (A or F)
2	Sales Revenue	25,550	26,888		
3	Direct Labour	16,000	17,512		
4	Direct Materials	2,995	2,875		
5	Administration Overheads	2,785	2,875		
6	Selling and Distribution Overheads	4,100	4,298		

(b) **Insert the formulas in the table below that you used in cells 2, 3, 4 and 5 of column D of the spreadsheet.**

	D
2	
3	
4	
5	

TASK 17

Shark Ltd has produced a performance report detailing budgeted and actual information for last month.

(a) **In column E identify significant variances in excess of 6% of budget, entering S for significant and NS for not significant. Variances should be calculated to two decimal places.**

	A	B	C	D	E
1	Cost Type	Budget £	Actual £	Variance £	Significant or Not Significant (S or NS)
2	Sales Revenue	160,000	165,400	5,400	
3	Direct Labour	45,000	47,500	2,500	
4	Direct Materials	22,700	21,200	1,500	
5	Administration Overheads	6,500	9,255	2,755	
6	Selling and Distribution Overheads	25,795	27,105	1,310	

(b) **Insert the variances from column D (cells D2 to D6 inclusive) in A→Z order in the table below.**

	D
2	
3	
4	
5	
6	

Section 4

MOCK EXAM ANSWERS

TASK 1

(a)

- True
- False
- False
- True

(b)

- True
- False
- False
- False

TASK 2

(a)

- Labour
- Material
- Overheads
- Overheads

(b)

- Direct
- Indirect
- indirect
- Direct

TASK 3

(a)

- Finance
- Production
- Admin
- Selling and distribution

(b)

- Variable
- Stepped
- Semi-variable
- Fixed

TASK 4

- A100
- B100
- B200
- C200
- A100
- B200

TASK 5

- IV100
- CO620
- RE300
- CO520
- CO720
- IV300

TASK 6

(a)

- Stepped
- Fixed
- Variable

(b)

- Fixed
- Fixed
- Variable

TASK 7

(a)

- Yes
- Yes
- No

(b)

Element	Unit Cost
Materials	£2.50
Labour	£16.00
Overheads	£11.20
Total	£29.70

TASK 8

Opening inventory of raw materials	6,000
Purchases of raw materials	22,000
Closing inventory of raw materials	6,400
DIRECT MATERIALS USED	
Direct Labour	45,000
DIRECT COST	
Manufacturing overheads	17,000
MANUFACTURING COST	
Opening inventory of work in progress	4,000
Closing inventory of work in progress	2,800
COST OF GOODS MANUFACTURED	
Opening inventory of finished goods	2,500
Closing inventory of finished goods	4,500
COST OF GOODS SOLD	

(b)

Cost	£
DIRECT MATERIALS USED	21,600
DIRECT COST	66,600
MANUFACTURING COST	83,600
COST OF GOODS MANUFACTURED	84,800
COST OF GOODS SOLD	82,800

TASK 9

(a)

- AVCO
- FIFO
- LIFO

(b)

- False
- False
- True

TASK 10

Method	Cost of Issue on July 22	Closing Stock at July 31
FIFO	£6,937.50	£12,162.50
LIFO	£6,912.50	£12,187.50
AVCO	£6,840.00	£12,260.00

TASK 11

(a)

- True
- True
- False

(b)

Worker	Hours Worked	Basic Wage	Overtime	Gross Wage
S. Illy	37 hours	£525	£45	£570
C. Razy	43 hours	£525	£180	£705

TASK 12

- True
- True
- False
- True

TASK 13

Day	Units made	Pay £
Monday	10	78
Tuesday	15	90
Wednesday	18	108
Thursday	9	78
Friday	20	120
Total weekly wage		474

TASK 14

(a)

Cell	Heading
B1	Sales
D1	Fixed costs
E1	Total costs

(b)

	A	B	C	D	E	F
1		?	Variable costs	?	?	Profit/(loss)
2	April	5,250	4,200	760	4,960	290
3	May	4,500	3,600	760	4,360	140
4	June	4,875	3,900	760	4,660	215
5	July	3,675	2,940	760	3,700	–25
6	Total	18,300	14,640	3,040	17,680	620

(c)

	A	B	C	D	F
6	Total	=sum(B2:B5)	=sum(C2:C5)	=sum(D2:D5	=sum(F2:F5)

OR

	A	B	C	D	F
6	Total	=B2+B3+B4+B5	=C2+C3+C4+ C5	=D2+D3+D4+D5	=F2+F3+F4+ F5

TASK 15

- True
- True
- True
- False

TASK 16

(a)

	A	B	C	D	E
1	Cost Type	Budget £	Actual £	Variance	Adverse or favourable (A or F)
2	Sales Revenue	25,550	26,888	£1,338	F
3	Direct Labour	16,000	17,512	£1,512	A
4	Direct Materials	2,995	2,875	£120	F
5	Administration Overheads	2,785	2,875	£90	A
6	Selling and Distribution Overheads	4,100	4,298	£198	A

(b)

	D
1	Variance
2	= C2 – B2 (or = B2 – C2)
3	= C3 – B3 (or = B3 – C3)
4	= C4 – B4 (or = B4 – C4)
5	= C5 – B5 (or = B5 – C5)

KAPLAN PUBLISHING

TASK 17

(a)

	A	B	C	D	E
1	Cost Type	Budget £	Actual £	Variance £	Significant or Not Significant (S or NS)
2	Sales Revenue	160,000	165,400	5,400	NS
3	Direct Labour	45,000	47,500	2,500	NS
4	Direct Materials	22,700	21,200	1,500	S
5	Administration Overheads	6,500	9,255	2,755	S
6	Selling and Distribution Overheads	25,795	27,105	1,310	NS

(b)

	D
2	1,310
3	1,500
4	2,500
5	2,755
6	5,400